Praise fo

"This is a gentle book full of humanity, biblical integrity and unexpected humour. It hums and brims with hard-won insights for those of us who wait for miracles, those who've given up waiting for miracles but would at least appreciate a few answers, and those who would simply like a little more hope.

"Helpfully designed for groups as well as individuals, I have no doubt that *Those Who Wait* will bring comfort, tears of relief and smiles of recognition to many, many people."

Pete Greig, author of *God on Mute: Engaging the Silence of Unanswered Prayer,* Spokesman for 24-7 Prayer International and Pastor of Emmaus Rd, Guildford

"Our culture says waiting is a waste, but our God says waiting is essential for faith. This book teaches us how to wait for the Lord. Through Marlow's imaginative retellings of the stories of Sarah, Isaiah, John the Baptist and Mary, readers of *Those Who Wait* will renew their strength, they will refresh their soul, and they will reconnect to their God."

David T. Lamb, author of *God Behaving Badly* and
Allan A. MacRae Professor of Old Testament, Biblical Theological Seminary

"Tanya Marlow has had to wait for years... and she is still waiting. From her background of chronic illness comes a book which lets the Scriptures fire your imagination as you enter into the faith journeys of four great ancient saints. The result will make her a cherished friend in print to countless readers, especially those who battle their own seemingly interminable struggles. What a blessing this book is!"

Mark Meynell, author of *A Wilderness of Mirrors* and *Cross-Examined* and Director of Langham Preaching, Europe and Caribbean

"Waiting is frustrating and painful, and there are few people who understand that. This book is a place to go to find support, to feel less alone and to be drawn into God's presence in the waiting. Beautiful, helpful and, most of all, encouraging."

Katharine Welby-Roberts, author of *I Thought There Would Be Cake*

"Out of her own experience of ongoing suffering, the author has written a reflection on four biblical characters that is unique and remarkable. The book is responsibly imaginative, beautifully written and readable, pastorally sensitive. Individuals and church groups will find it very helpful and a great resource."

Dr David Wenham, author of *The Parables of Jesus,*
New Testament Tutor and Former Vice Principal of Trinity College, Bristol

"Tanya Marlow weaves the universal experience of waiting, all its frustrations, pains and hopes, into four retellings of biblical stories. Her imagination and creativity allow the stories to illumine our waiting, our times of darkness and doubt. The follow-up activities deepen the experience. The stories made me cry and made me smile. Gentle but unflinchingly honest, this is a book full of love, faith and hope, facing pain with open eyes. Read it to be encouraged, read it to be challenged, read it to be comforted."

Dr Jenni Williams, author of *God Remembered Rachel*
and Tutor in Old Testament, Wycliffe Hall, University of Oxford

"Tanya Marlow has given us a creative, engaging and timely gift that addresses the universal challenge of waiting on God. Framed with her own health struggles and written with a novelist's attention to detail, readers will find Marlow a reliable and refreshing guide through uncertain seasons of life."

Ed Cyzewski, author of *A Christian Survival Guide* and *Flee, Be Silent, Pray*

"Tanya Marlow's words sent me both to my journal and to my knees. While her body is mainly house-bound, her words are filled with an expansive spirit. *Those Who Wait* is such a beautiful invitation to connect with our longing, our hope, our honesty and the God who meets us in the waiting."

Idelette McVicker, Founder of *SheLovesMagazine.com*

"What shall we do during the waiting? How can God redeem it? Tanya Marlow explores these questions in her engaging look at four biblical characters who had to wait. She brings their stories to life, all the while imbuing hope and strength in those of us who wait. Which is everyone, I reckon. Don't miss it."

Amy Boucher Pye, author of *Finding Myself in Britain*

"Writing from her own experiences of suffering, Tanya gently reminds us that we are not alone. Through her eyes we are reminded of God's kindness and faithfulness, and she introduces us afresh to familiar Bible characters and truth. This is a beautiful book – full of heartache, but also hope."

Emma Scrivener, author of *A New Name* and *A New Day*

"I would recommend this book to anyone who is currently in a season of waiting - whether waiting for healing, waiting for restoration of relationships, or waiting for a dream to be fulfilled. Ultimately, it is a book for all of us, as we wrestle with the kingdom of now and not yet, seeking to live well in the unanswered pains and sorrows of life, awaiting the promise of what is to come."

Becky Drake, Christian songwriter and Founder of Worship for Everyone

THOSE WHO
WAIT

FINDING GOD IN DISAPPOINTMENT, DOUBT AND DELAY

Tanya Marlow

malcolm down
PUBLISHING

Those Who Wait: Finding God in Disappointment, Doubt and Delay

21 20 19 18 17   7 6 5 4 3 2 1

First published in 2017 by Malcolm Down Publishing Ltd.
www.malcolmdown.co.uk

ISBN 978-1-910786-86-4

Cover Image © Jon Marlow 2017 marlow.me.uk
Cover Design © Laura Pasterfield-Ferguson 2017
LauraSFerguson.wixsite.com/mysite

Tanya Marlow is a writer, speaker and broadcaster on faith and spirituality. She writes about the Bible, the messy edges of life and finding God in unexpected places at tanyamarlow.com. For news, exclusive offers and a free gift, sign up at: tinyurl.com/tanyamarlowwaits

For Jenny "J K" Rowbory,
poet extraordinaire;
whose life and character
while waiting for more than a decade in isolation and pain
have inspired and sustained me,
and who shows me Christ, every single day.
With love and penguin poo

www.jkrowbory.co.uk

Contents

Foreword by Addie Zierman   Page 9

INTRODUCTION CHAPTERS

1. The Wait of the World   Page 12
2. How to Use this Book   Page 20
3. To Begin - The Clock   Page 22
4. Trigger Warning (infertility, rape)   Page 24

SECTION ONE: SARAH'S STORY
Dealing with Disappointment - Waiting for Joy

Prelude to Sarah   Page 26
1. The Call (Genesis 12:1-9)   Page 27
2. The Fear (Genesis 12:10-20)   Page 31
3. The Longing (Genesis 17:1-27)   Page 37
4. The Visitors (Genesis 18:1-15)   Page 41
5. The Laughter (Genesis 21:1-7)   Page 46
6. Sarah - General Reflections   Page 49

SECTION TWO: ISAIAH'S STORY
Dealing with Delay - Waiting for Justice and Peace

Prelude to Isaiah   Page 54
1. How Long, O Lord? (Isaiah 6:1-13)   Page 55
2. The Short Wait for Immanuel (Isaiah 7:1-25)   Page 61
3. Baz and the Short Wait for War (Isaiah 8:1-18)   Page 67
4. The Long Wait for Light (Isaiah 9:1-7)   Page 73
5. The Long Wait for Peace (Isaiah 10:33-11:9)   Page 78
6. Isaiah - General Reflections   Page 83

SECTION THREE: JOHN THE BAPTIST'S STORY
Dealing with Doubt - Waiting for Your Life's Calling

Prelude to John the Baptist   Page 88
1. The Disappointment (Luke 1:57-80)   Page 89
2. The Destroyer (Luke 3:1-14)   Page 94
3. The Doubter (Luke 3:15-22)   Page 98
4. The Greatest (Matthew 11:2-15)   Page 103
5. The Least (Mark 6:17-29)   Page 108
6. John - General Reflections   Page 113

SECTION FOUR: MARY, MOTHER OF JESUS' STORY
Dealing with Disgrace - Waiting for Jesus

Prelude to Mary   Page 118
1. When Heaven Waits (Luke 1:26-38)   Page 119
2. Waiting for Reassurance (Luke 1:39-56)   Page 124
3. Waiting for Mercy (Matthew 1:18-25)   Page 130
4. Waiting to Arrive (Luke 2:1-7)   Page 135
5. Waiting for the Pain to Stop (Luke 2:7, Romans 8:18-26)   Page 140
6. Mary - General Reflections   Page 144

SECTION FIVE: THE GOD WHO WAITS

1. The God Who Waits   Page 148
2. A Benediction for Those Who Wait   Page 155
3. A Benediction for Times of Advent   Page 157
4. Whole Book - Summary and Reflections   Page 159

APPENDIX A: THEOLOGICAL CHOICES AND HISTORICAL NOTES

1. Notes for Sarah's Story   Page 164
2. Notes for Isaiah's Story   Page 170
3. Notes for John's Story   Page 180
4. Notes for Mary's Story   Page 184

APPENDIX B: SIX BIBLE STUDIES

How to use the Bible Studies   Page 190

1. The Wait of the World   Page 192
Being Patient - James 5:7-11

2. Sarah   Page 196
Scarred Souls and Hospitable Hearts - Genesis 18:1-15

3 Isaiah   Page 201
How Long, O Lord? - Isaiah 6:1-13

4 John the Baptist   Page 206
Receiving Your Life as a Gift - John 3:22-30

5 Mary   Page 210
Belonging and Isolation - Luke 1:39-55

6 The God Who Waits   Page 214
We Do Not Groan Alone - Romans 8:18-28

Select Bibliography   Page 217
Acknowledgements   Page 219
About the Author   Page 223

Foreword

I am sitting on a couch that is not mine, in a home that is not mine, on a grey September Monday.

Waiting.

The house that I'm in right now belongs to my in-laws, as does the grey and white floral rug under my feet, the white kitchen cabinets where I keep shoving our various groceries, and the dark brown wood floors that show off the millions of crumbs that seem to appear whenever either of my kids eats so much as a peanut.

Here's what happened: in July, we put our suburban home of ten years on the market, hoping to find a place a little farther into the country. It felt to me, as I sat on the deck, like this was *the next right thing,* the direction toward which God was nodding toward, and I e-signed my signature on all the right forms without too much fuss.

Within days, we'd found the perfect house: a little white country charmer with a pond and a chicken coop and a wide front porch.

We made an offer. We didn't get it.

We kept looking, and eventually, we found another lovely house. Not as awesome as the first, but still good. Within days I had mentally furnished the yard with a plucky group of chickens and dreamed up several things we could do with that big, red barn.

But we didn't get that house, either.

In the meantime, our home sold in a record four days, and we spent the month cleaning and packing and turning nervous eyes back to Zillow again and again, until it became apparent that we were going to be a little bit homeless if we didn't figure something out.

Which is how I found myself here, in my in-laws' living room, where I am both extremely grateful, and extremely stressed about wrecking the rug – in equal measures.

I have waited for things in my life. I've waited for love and for direction and for some shock of divine presence in a season of doubt. I've waited for babies that didn't come and for the ones that did and for a book contract that was both a dream come true and *not* a dream come true, all at once.

Now I find myself in this liminal *in between* space again, and it comes like muscle memory: the doubt and the pain, the anger and the guilt, the questions and fears and exhaustion. The *Where are you, God?*, the wakeful nights, the feeling that I must have misheard somehow or I wouldn't be *here*. Again.

I'd forgotten how lonely the waiting feels. But of course, waiting is an absolutely universal experience. Normal. Maybe even essential, in that mysterious, divine space where God is at work.

In this beautiful book, Tanya Marlow reminds us of just this.

With grace and candour, Tanya imbues the stories of four familiar biblical characters with her own intimate experience of waiting on God. And her authenticity acts as a kind of seasoning, bringing forth flavours of their lives that had been lost, at least for me, in the hundreds of readings and sermons and retellings I've heard over the years.

These stories, paired with Tanya's gentle reflection questions and prayers, remind me that waiting is hard for *everyone*. But it is also formational and beautiful and purposeful in ways I can't always understand. They invite me to interact with my grief and pain and fear, but not to forget that God is good, and his ways are higher than mine.

Whatever you find yourself waiting for right now, may you find comfort and companionship in these stories. You are connected to a great company of those who have waited and are waiting, surrounded by the love of Immanuel, *God with us,* the One who waits with us all.

Addie Zierman,
author of *When We Were on Fire* and *Night Driving*

INTRODUCTION
The Wait of the World

1. The Wait of the World

To wait is the human condition. Or, as the wise philosopher Dr Seuss once wrote, "Everyone is just...waiting".[1]

We spend our lives waiting, yet we all hate to wait.

Everyone can sit patiently for a short time. The last time I was at a doctor's appointment, I sat in the waiting room with calm breathing and a beatific smile. That state of serenity lasted approximately twenty seconds.

I guess others can manage longer than me, but - truly - experiments have shown that some people, left alone in an empty room for just fifteen minutes, would rather give themselves painful electric shocks than spend time waiting.[2]

Even waiting for a few minutes is uncomfortable and discomfiting. Checking your text messages or emails for a reply that hasn't come; sitting on your bag, with no bus in sight; twiddling your thumbs until the appointment time: these are the background irritations of the little-waits.

Waiting on a long-term basis is of another order entirely. To be in a long-term state of limbo, not knowing the outcome or length of time waiting, is utterly, shatteringly exhausting.

What Am I Waiting For?

When I was a kid, I waited for a toy A La Carte Kitchen every Christmas for four years. (It never came.)

But the big wait of my life has been my health.

In my teens, I had a bad case of glandular fever (mononucleosis), which later morphed into a neurological illness: myalgic encephalomyelitis (ME). At first, it was just muscle pain and exhaustion, falling asleep in the middle of the day, unable to concentrate for long. Later, my balance and mobility were affected.

---

[1] From the children's book: Dr Seuss, *Oh, the Places You'll Go!*, Random House, 1990. It's a classic. Read it - you'll thank me.

[2] See Wilson, T. D., Reinhard, D. A., Westgate, E. C., Gilbert, D. T., Ellerbeck, N., Hahn, C., et al. (2014). Just think: the challenges of the disengaged mind. *Science* 345, 75–77. doi: 10.1126/science.1250830

It took me ten years, and many dismissive doctors, for my condition to be diagnosed.

ME is a disease with an unknown prognosis. Of the 250,000 in UK with the illness, I may be one of the few who make a full recovery, one of the majority who experience some improvement, or one of the quarter of patients who deteriorate, never recovering. Because of how my illness progressed, the odds are not in my favour, yet there is still that sliver of hope of recovery.

After the diagnosis, I assumed my illness was temporary and waited to recover. I took a part-time job, expecting it to be full-time in a couple of years. But after two years, I was using a wheelchair and not able to work at all.

My husband, Jon, and I waited longer for me to get better, delaying having a child. One day we could wait no more. I wanted children, even if it risked worsening my health - which, sadly, it did, and on a scale we weren't expecting. For months after childbirth I was too ill to change my baby's nappies or walk from one end of the hall to the other. My legs collapsed after a few paces.

Again, we had no way of knowing whether this new disability would be temporary or permanent. We hoped it would be temporary, and waited for my health to improve before trying for more children. We waited - weeks, months, years - for significant improvement.

I'm still waiting.

I've improved, but not by much. At the time of writing, I have been housebound for seven years, only able to leave the house once a fortnight for a few blissful hours out in a wheelchair. I exist mainly in bed.

In those hours alone, I wait for recovery: the freedom to play in the park with my son or go to friends' houses for dinner. I wait to be able to run. I wait to be able to go to church. I wait to be able to help Jon with the washing up. (Admittedly, that last one's not at the top of the list.)

It's been over twenty years since I went to the doctor with a sore throat as a teenager. We've adjusted to our new lives, but we're still in limbo. We wobble at the top of a balance point that could bring either recovery or further disability, not knowing in which direction we will fall.

Sometimes I wait for better health like an irritated adult, struggling against the awkwardness and discomfort of waiting. Sometimes I wait like a preschool child on the way to the beach, yelling to God repeatedly, "Are we nearly there yet?", whining and fidgeting when the answer comes back "Not yet", infuriated by its vagueness. Often I wait with peace - or resignation (it can be hard to distinguish between the two). Sometimes I wait with secret hope.

What Are You Waiting For?

There are the usual categories that spring to mind: waiting for a career; a spouse; a child; healing from mental or physical illnesses. But there are also more nebulous longings. We wait:

~ to know who we truly are and what our purpose is;
~ to feel like we have enough time to give all our commitments justice;
~ for our debts to be paid;
~ for respect and recognition;
~ for the abusive person to be out of our life;
~ to feel like we belong;
~ to feel loved and accepted as we are;
~ for security;
~ for reassurance that we're doing okay;
~ for the loneliness to pass;
~ for our addiction to stop ruling us;
~ for the freedom to do what we love, not what we have to do;
~ for a real home;
~ for a little more time;
~ for justice in the world;
~ to stop feeling emotional pain, or - superstitiously - waiting for the day that we stop being happy and our world will crumble.

Behind every wish that we'd get a hospital appointment soon, there's a wish to remain healthy. Behind that wish to be healthy is a desire to live forever with healed, whole bodies. When we're waiting for the kids to stop fighting, we are also waiting for an end to all wars. While we wait for a promotion, we're also waiting to be respected and known entirely, using our gifts for the glory of God.

We spend our lives waiting.

Even our little waitings echo the tensions of the bigger waits, which in turn reveal the longest wait of the world. Humanity writhes and cries out against suffering, death, and sickness. Deep in our core, we long for wholeness, heaven and the incomparable beauty of seeing Jesus face to face.

We wait for Jesus. We can't help it.

Waiting is sewn into our existence, and we have plenty of practice at it. Theoretically, we should be good at it.

But we hate to wait. It's a rare person who simply submits to a period of waiting; we wrestle it with every fibre of our being.

Why? Because we have a God-given instinct to want to know the end of the story, and for that ending to be good.

Why We Hate Waiting

Waiting is uncertain

If you knew that you were going to be unemployed for exactly thirteen months before landing a well-paid job, and you had enough money to live on in the meantime, you could spend that time relaxing. Maybe you could volunteer at a soup kitchen, travel around the world or fulfil your lifelong wish to play the cello. Unfortunately, unemployment doesn't tell you when it's going to end or when you will next have money coming in. You're constantly having to push doors and read rejection letters, and that's not quite so much fun as playing the cello. Likewise, if you were desperate to be married, but somehow knew for sure you would be married to the love of your life at the age of forty, the decades of singleness beforehand would be easier to handle.

Waiting reminds us we are not fully in control of our lives

Modern city life is full of noise and distraction, and we are unfamiliar with stillness. For those of us who live ordered and settled lives, a season of waiting can be a time of crisis. To wait, without knowing how long we have to wait or what the outcome will be, can be a crushing reminder that we don't have full control over our lives. We plot our steps, but we can't guarantee our future. A season of waiting brings us face to face with ourselves in solitude. We want to block the reality of our relative helplessness, so we reach for distractions to stop the discomfort.

Waiting causes you to doubt yourself

When I am in a doctor's waiting room, I have an irrational fear that they will have called my name and I won't have noticed. Just at the point when I am fully absorbed in last year's celebrity scandal or a beautiful woman who dropped three dress sizes in two weeks and ran a marathon five minutes after giving birth, I look up, guiltily, convinced I have heard someone mention my name. This is when my Britishness conspires against me, because I want to make sure that I haven't missed my appointment (which would be awkward); however, I don't want to ask the receptionist if they've called my name in case they haven't, making me look belligerent (which would be very awkward).

Likewise, in a period of extended waiting in life, it is all too easy to assume that something is wrong. We assume that 'something' is us.

We have been waiting too long; it cannot be right.

Maybe it's our fault. Perhaps we missed a cue somewhere. Maybe it's because we haven't tried the infertility acupuncture. Perhaps if we made more effort, our estranged father would respond reasonably this time. Maybe we should have gone for that job in Scotland, after all. Maybe we didn't pray hard enough for healing.

Waiting means continually trying to keep your balance

Even in a doctor's waiting room, you cannot properly flick through the trashy magazines, because you have one ear on the announcements and one eye on the clock, watching the minutes tick further past your allotted appointment time. To wait means you are constantly straddling two realities - the hoped-for outcome either happening, or not. Yes, or no. Yes, or no. You feel the pull of both possibilities as you wait.

Amy Young, in her excellent book *Looming Transitions,* illustrates this experience.[3] Picture a pyramid. At the top of the pyramid, see a ball, balancing on the tip. The ball doesn't want to stay balanced at the top. It wants to run down one side, or another. Any side will do.

Likewise, at some point, your hope yields to a disappointed resignation. It's the only way to cope. After months or years of waiting for a loving family or the job you so desperately need, it becomes easier to imagine life without the longed-for outcome rather than holding those two possibilities at once. It's easier for the ball to run down the side of disappointment than to stay at the top in limbo.

This is why, in a period of extended waiting, we often go through many different emotions: initial patience; hope; irritation; insecurity; major tantrum; doubt; helplessness; despair - and eventual submission to the status quo. Some are able to hang onto hope, but that's often emotionally exhausting in itself.

To be in a period of waiting is stressful, uncertain, exhausting and profoundly discomfiting.

There is good news, however:

---

[3] Amy Young, *Looming Transitions: Starting and Finishing Well in Cross-Cultural Service*, Createspace, 2015

Waiting ends eventually, and sometimes your dreams are realised

It's like being in a doctor's waiting room for so long that you've almost forgotten what you're doing there. You have given up waiting, and you're fully engrossed in following the five rules for last year's summer fashion, when - suddenly - your name is called. Even though it's what you were waiting for all along, it comes like a rude interruption to life. You've forgotten everything: the speech you had rehearsed for the doctor; the symptoms you'd listed in your head. It's finally come after all this time and, paradoxically, you now feel utterly unprepared.

When the waiting ends, even if it's planned, it always feels like a surprise.

How Should We Wait?

My struggle with health got me thinking: what is the 'Christian' way to wait? Or indeed, are there many Christian ways of waiting? How did the characters in the Bible wait for years before they saw God's promises to them realised? What about those promised something who never saw it come to fruition?

Sometimes we forget they were real people, not fictional saints. I reminded myself that these characters in Scripture actually existed, and asked myself some questions. How might real people in these situations react? What were the Bible characters thinking and feeling? Where was God in it all?

This book is the result of that exploration: four stories of ordinary heroes who wrestled with waiting but found God there. It has a twin focus: waiting for God's specific promises but also ultimately awaiting Christ's coming (for them), and Christ's return (for us).

Sarah: Dealing with Disappointment - Waiting for joy

"I wanted fulfilment: instead, God repeated the promise.
"I cling to the words, but sometimes I feel as if my whole life has been a long wandering, a long hunger that hasn't yet been satisfied." - Sarah's Story

How do you cope when your prayers go unanswered? As we wait with Sarah for a home and family, we walk through long-term disappointment to ultimate joy.

Isaiah: Dealing with Delay - Waiting for justice and peace

"I would be grateful for another sign-child: one who proclaimed peace, not disaster. Perhaps they will come. But probably not in my lifetime." - Isaiah's Story

How do we deal with longings, not just for ourselves but the wider world? Isaiah lived in a time of great upheaval and global uncertainty; with him we wait for ultimate peace and justice.

John: Dealing with Doubt - Waiting for your life's purpose

"Time went on, and still I waited to become something I wasn't. Everywhere I turned, I was disappointing someone." - John the Baptist's Story

How do you find the true purpose of your life? John waited twice: once to enter his life's calling, and again as he waited in prison for freedom or death. With him, we wrestle with doubt.

Mary: Dealing with Disgrace - Waiting for Jesus

"This was the moment humanity had been waiting for: the Saviour appearing, wrinkled and new." - Mary's Story

What does it look like to wait for Jesus? Mary had the shortest wait for Christ, but she waited as an outsider, rejected by society. For us, Mary's pregnancy and labour help us meditate on Christ's Second Coming.

Issues of Interpretation

In recreating the Bible stories, I had to make interpretative choices. For example: the Bible says Jesus was born in an animal's feeding trough. Did that mean he was born in a stable? Or a cave, such as the ones in Bethlehem, which probably housed animals? Or was it a trough in the open air by a field? Or the bottom floor of an ordinary house, where animals were tethered? There are scholarly arguments for any and all of these interpretations.

In sermons and devotional books, the preacher can show their research and give you three valid options. But in a story, you can't say, 'Then Mary went to a field, or maybe a cave, stable or house, and gave birth there'. This is not a Choose Your Own Adventure Story. I had to pick what I judged to be the most likely option, using research and my imagination. (This is the fun part of being an author: the sheer power of it all.) The narrative contextualization for Isaiah's life in prophecies of Isaiah 1-11 is scarce, so that section takes more liberties than the others.

For those who like to know why I made the choices I did and how much was from my imagination, research or the Bible text, I have included thorough notes for each section at the back of the book.

Everyone builds up a different picture about biblical characters from the information we've been given in the Bible and from films, art and nativity plays. This is mine.

My aim is to make the familiar stories a little unfamiliar to us again, so we rediscover the Bible anew. As the read, I imagine there will be moments when you ask, 'Why did she interpret it that way? I don't like it! Is it right?' I welcome these questions, and my hope is that, rather than moving away from the Bible text, these creative pieces will urge us back into the text with fresh questions and insight.

Those Who Wait

This book is for those who are waiting, which is all of us. It's for those who struggle with waiting, which is most of us.

It's for the impatient, questioning, twitching or angry wait-ers who feel like we're losing sight of God in it all. It's for those whose lives are so full we forget we're participating in the longest wait of history.

I'm inviting you to put down some of the distractions and lean into the discomfort of waiting. It's not an obviously attractive invitation, I'll admit: "Come and have some discomfort! ...Anyone??"

But counter-intuitively, these stories show us that God turns up in our discomfort - and that makes all the difference. Through revisiting and entering into these stories, it is my hope and prayer that we would also meet with God.

2. How to Use this Book

The book is mainly story, designed to help us recover the excitement and tension of the Bible, so you may want to gobble it up in one gulp. It's equally suitable for use as a slower devotional or group study.

Here are some suggestions of how to do it:

Personal Devotion

For each of the four Bible characters, there are five first-person narrative episodes of their life, comprising the creative retelling plus a couple of reflection questions: twenty chapters in all. These chapters work well as personal devotions or a very short group study. At the end of each character's story, there is an additional sixth chapter, with some reflection questions and suggestions for prayer. Some of the suggestions for prayer are repeated in the Bible studies.

Group Study and Discussion

If you are working through the book with others, use the six group Bible studies that accompany the book instead of the general reflection chapters, as they contain some of the same exercises. You can find the Bible studies towards the back of the book.

Use it in corporate worship

Excerpts from the book would make good dramatic readings, and the reflection questions, creative exercises and prayer suggestions lend themselves to creative or informal services.

The stories are a suitable adjunct for Bible studies or sermon series on the characters' lives.

Reading the Book in Advent

In the midst of jingly carols and endless nativity plays, we have lost the original, traditional observance of the season of Advent. It's intended to be a season of waiting. Advent means 'arrival'. The season divides history into two periods of waiting: for the first coming (incarnation) and second coming (return) of the Christ.

In fact, I structured the book around the tradition of lighting the Advent candle wreath. Though traditions vary, in the Church of England the four candles of the Advent wreath represent the patriarchs (Abraham, Isaac, Jacob), then the Prophets, with John the Baptist and Mary, mother of Jesus, following as immediate forerunners to Jesus. I chose Sarah as 'matriarch' and chose Isaiah to represent 'The Prophets' candle.

Option One - Daily Advent Calendar

~ In November, read the Introduction Chapters.
~ Then, read one chapter a day in December (including either the short Reflection chapters or the full group Bible study every 6th day). This gives you 24 chapters, taking you up to December 24th, Christmas Eve.
~ Read the Epilogue: 'The God Who Waits', on or after Christmas Day.

Option Two - The Advent Wreath Calendar

~ The idea of this is to coordinate with the Advent wreath.
~ Count back five Sundays before Christmas Day to the Sunday before Advent. (This may be in November.) Read the Introduction Chapters that Sunday.
~ The next day, start reading Sarah's story, reading a chapter a day, with Sundays off. If you continue in this pattern and your church follows this tradition, you should find that the relevant candle is lit after you have read each story.

3. To Begin

These exercises are also included in the first Bible study if you wish to do the group discussion instead of private processing.

Before you jump into the stories, take a minute to slow down and think through your own journey.

The Clock - What are you waiting for?

On a blank piece of paper, draw a small clock.

Think about all the areas of your life where you feel 'liminal': in-between, unfulfilled, in limbo. (Look back through the suggestions in the Introduction Chapters if you need a prompt.)

Around the clock, write down everything in your life that you are waiting for, from the 'little waitings' to the 'big waits'.

This can be a surprisingly vulnerable exercise.

Keep this clock somewhere prominent while you work through this book, as a reminder of all you're waiting for.

Creative Exercise - The Practice of Waiting

For however long it takes you to work through this book, whenever you find yourself waiting, (perhaps for an appointment or in a traffic jam), try not to pick up your phone or book; don't distract yourself at all. Instead, sit with the silence and the discomfort awhile. Aim to spend at least fifteen minutes pausing each day, even if your day feels full.

~ What do you feel when you wait like this?
~ What does it tell you about yourself? And about God?

Invite God into those conscious times of waiting. Perhaps God will speak, perhaps there will be silence - what matters is making space.

Prayer Suggestions for Those Who Wait

Dear Lord, I am waiting [to/for]
[pause to name aloud or silently the waiting situation you shared in the clock exercise].

You came to earth as a weak human.
You will come again in glory as a powerful King.
In between these times,
Please come afresh into my life.
I invite you into my frustration, my excitement;
My disappointment, my hope.

Let me know your empathy as a God-born-baby;
In control of the universe, yet helpless and flailing.
Let me know your power as a good ruler
Who acts at just the right time and comes to make everything right.
Remind me of the good beginning and the good ending.

Lord, be with me in the middle of my story.
Bring me perspective, and let me see your purpose in the waiting.
While I wait, give me endurance and strength to hold fast to you.
Lord Jesus Christ, would you come to me today.
Amen

Breath-prayers for Seasons of Waiting

Use these as prayers for when you can't pray, those moments when your deferred dreams are too much to handle. Pray these as often as you need in the days or weeks that you work through this book.

~ "Please, Lord, be with me in the waiting, be present in my confusion."
~ "O Lord, lift up my head."
~ "Spirit, please take my burden."
~ "Lord Jesus, refresh my hope and give me peace."
~ "I wait for the Lord, my whole being waits; and in his word I put my hope." (Psalm 130:5)
~ "Lord, I wait for you; you will answer, Lord my God." (Psalm 38:15)

4. Trigger Warning

Sarah's story describes in detail the experience of suffering infertility for years, eventually having a baby. This story, especially chapters 4 and 5, plus chapter 5 of Mary's story, which describes labour, may be hard for some to read, especially if the wounds of loss and disappointment are raw. Pregnancy is also used as a metaphor in the epilogue.

Sarah's story contains the threat of rape (chapter 2), which could trigger trauma for some.

SECTION ONE
Sarah's Story

Dealing with Disappointment
Waiting for Joy

Prelude to Sarah's Story

From the dawn of the world, travel forward in time. Since the world's first murder, when Cain ran away in disgrace, the world has been rolling for approximately two thousand years. Noah has long since survived the flood, and the world is now a civilised place, with laws and cities and bustling trade. In the centre of this busy world of thousands of inhabitants there lived one ordinary, long-suffering wife, doing her laundry. Her name, at least at this point, was Sarai.

1. The Call
Sarah's Story (Genesis 12:1-9)

I laughed at my husband. I thought he was joking.

"Why would we move again?" I asked him, but it was a rhetorical question; I didn't wait for an answer. I was busy washing the linen at the time, submerging my robe into a bucket by the stream, trying to get rid of the pomegranate stain. I didn't even turn around, didn't break rhythm with the scrubbing. We'd already had one major move when Abram's ageing father had the bright idea of upping sticks from Ur and moving to Canaan.

Canaan was the plan, anyway, but health problems delayed us, so we stopped after a while and settled in this town, Harran. It was still a big city, but smaller than Ur. Both cities honoured the moon god, which was what Abram's father wanted, so it all felt familiar. It was nice enough. There was room for all the family to be there without being under each other's feet; we had shade, a stream, the market nearby - everything was set up perfectly. Abram and I preferred it to the crowded streets of Ur, where we had grown up.

We'd done the big move of our lives, and I felt settled here. We had roots here: friends, family, a solid income. There was no way we would be moving again - everything we needed was here. Abram was joking, I assumed. Though, come to think of it, it wasn't a very funny joke.

The sun was shining brightly that morning, and tiny purple flowers by the stream had emerged from their winter sleep. I took the robe out of the water and examined it: the stain was still there. With a sigh, I tipped the water into the stream, refilled the bucket and plunged the robe back in. The water was freezing. I glanced behind me; Abram was still standing there, hovering awkwardly.

***

We were practically family already, even before we got married. I counted myself lucky when my father announced Abram would be my husband, and I had nodded with relief. My memories of childhood centre around long autumn nights, celebrating the harvest with countless aunts, uncles, first, second and third cousins. The adults would drink wine, the men laughing with the men, the women laughing with the women, while we kids roamed free, chasing each other in the stubbly field. Sometimes, when we had exhausted ourselves, we huddled together in one big group and looked up at the stars, inventing names for the star-clusters we could trace in the sky.

Even as children, we had teased one another, squabbled together, played, schemed and dreamed. I thought I knew everything there was to know about Abram. But then today he had announced his great plan to leave our home, our friends, our family - everything - and live miles away in a foreign country.

So I had laughed at him.

"I'm serious, Sarai," he said, and there was something about his tone that stopped my laughter. I stilled my hands, and the water ceased bubbling and subdued to a strange calm as he stood beside me. There he was: my husband, grey-haired and leathered by years in the sun, but with a new spark in his eyes. My stomach tightened, though whether it was with excitement or dread I couldn't tell you.

"Leave? Your father would never agree to that," I said, shaking off the water from my hand. "And we couldn't leave without his blessing - we couldn't abandon him when he's the head of our family. They'd never speak to us again. In fact, all our friends would probably avoid us. We'd be the disgrace of the whole town. Everywhere we went, people would wonder where our family was."

I waited for his laughter and for the whole idea to be dismissed. There were standards to be kept, morals to be respected. But he just nodded slowly, as if he'd already thought of that.

"God - the Creator-God - spoke to me," he said, by way of explanation. "Prepare yourself for huge news! We - and our future family - will be part of the true God's plan to bless the whole world."

In the distance, I could hear the shout of children playing while clouds hovered above us. Life was going on as normal, but it felt as though the air had stilled around us, as though we were in a silent bubble.

I knew the stories, of course - Noah, the tower of Babel, all that. But growing up in Ur, with moon idols on sale everywhere you turned, plus the huge choice of other gods in the surrounding towns, it was easy to forget the God of our ancestors. My father-in-law, Terah, was keen to fit in and went religiously to the temple of Nanna, but Abram and I had always held off, though others mocked us for being old-fashioned, or occasionally condemned us for being disloyal, antisocial.

I paused to consider Abram's words. This Creator-God seemed different to the other gods, especially when Abram described their encounter. This was a god who communicated through words, not just with symbols or harvest crops; a god of peace rather than warring with deities and humanity.

The Lord was more personable, more real than the other gods. Even as Abram was saying the words, I knew within my heart that he really had met with God and heard those promises. I knew it was true: I just wasn't sure I liked it.

Turning my back to him, I started scrubbing again, and I said nothing. The stain would not come out. My hands were red with the cold, and I was aching from the effort, but I would not stop scrubbing.

It wasn't just the immensity of the promises that frightened me - being chosen by this Creator God, the new land, blessing all peoples of the earth - it was the word 'family'. For so long I had been waiting for the blessing of a baby, feeling the ache in my empty womb. I stopped that thought as quickly as it started; I could not think about that hope, not after all these years. It was too painful.

A cloud covered the sun, and the air was suddenly colder. Abram remained standing behind me, unmoving, quiet.

"What about our family here? Are we to uproot them all?" I asked, looking straight ahead at those purple flowers. "How many would come with us? This will upset the whole family. What about all our nieces and nephews who have been children for us when we have been denied that pleasure?"

These grand promises were all very well, but I couldn't touch them, I couldn't see them. This stream: this is what I could see in front of me. This is what we would lose: our home, our family - my everything.

I felt the emotion rising in my cheeks, so I redoubled the scrubbing. With every movement, I decided I would try not to think about it too much. Maybe it was a word from God, maybe it wasn't. Maybe it was a belated mid-life crisis.

Abram stayed behind me, and it was his turn to be silent. Perhaps he is thinking of our own children, I thought. Perhaps he is thinking that it's worth the sacrifice if we have all these children of our own. But how? How? It was a medical impossibility.

"I want to be sure," I said, quietly. I wasn't sure exactly who I was saying it to - whether it was to him, or to God. It wasn't that it didn't excite me. I was thirsty for blessing, my spirit longing to know the Creator more. But I wanted to be sure I could hope for a future for us before we ripped away from our past. Abram kept silent, and I wondered if God was silent on this question, too.

I looked at the robe: the stain was still there. I sighed and squeezed the water out, then I tipped the contents of the bucket away. I turned around and met his gaze.

"Okay," I said. There was something in me that knew it was the right thing to do. If the Lord calls, you go. It's just what you do. "Let's go."

Abram put his arm around me and grinned, as if he had known all along that I would come round, and we strolled back together to where the rest of the family were eating.

We started packing that very night.

To reflect on:

"The Lord had said to Abram, "Go from your country, your people, and your father's household to the land I will show you.

"I will make you into a great nation,
and I will bless you;
I will make your name great,
and you will be a blessing.
I will bless those who bless you,
and whoever curses you I will curse;
and all peoples on earth
will be blessed through you."

Genesis 12:1-3

For further reading:

Genesis 12: 1-9

Over to you:

1. "...a god who communicated through words, not just with symbols or harvest crops." What are the different idols we see today that cause us to forget God? What are the things in your life that make it harder to hear from God?

2. "If God calls, you go." When have you felt the call of God in your life before? (This includes not just 'Big' callings like Abram and Sarai's but any nudge from God to change direction in your life.)

3. "Go from your country, your people and your father's household" (Gen 12:1). To obey God, Abram left his land, his community and even much of his family. Have you ever sacrificed comfort and security for the sake of obedience? What did you lose? What did you gain?

2. The Fear
Sarah's Story (Genesis 12:10-20)

This is not how the story was supposed to go. This much I knew. We had left everything back in Harran for the promise of amazing land and millions of children, but it had turned into an everlasting journey. Moreh, Shechem, Bethel, Ai, Negev - really, I would have been happy if we'd settled in any of these places, but Abram always looked restless and said it wasn't the right one yet.

Then came the drought. It was a bad one, and we were already living with meagre provisions which dwindled further by the day. We waited a few days, then a few weeks, praying for rain. After a while, we grew desperate; we had to follow a path back to food.

So here we were, on the road to Egypt, on a pilgrimage to find food. I had a vague sense of foreboding throughout the journey. We were short of water and, as the dust swirled around us, my tongue grew thicker and grainier. I didn't say much, because I couldn't - my mind was cloudy with hunger. Abram, however, chattered wildly the whole time and didn't seem quite himself.

I was aware of his fear at the back of my mind, but - the hunger. When you're that hungry, it's hard to think straight. My body and mind were fading, my concentration drifting in and out. All I could do was focus on staying on this lumbering animal. It was taking an eternity to get to our destination.

By the time we staggered to Pharaoh's grand stone palace, the famous giant pyramids looming over us in the distance, I felt paper-thin and shaky, only aware of the smell of roasted cattle and the lightness of my head.

If I had been more alert, I would have seen Abram's shuffling feet, his wringing hands. As it was, he ambushed me twenty seconds before our host greeted us, and he muttered, "Say you're my sister, not my wife."

"Say I'm not your wife," I repeated, with confusion.

"They're wicked idol-worshippers here. You're so beautiful - they'll kill me if you don't. They might kill you as well."

I looked at his eyes, and I saw his fear. In that split-second moment, I said yes.

I was tired and hungry, and I wanted him to love me, so I said yes.

***

Men at the table had surrounded me and were touching my hair, admiring my figure, commenting on my height. Unsure of my position, I froze under their touch but wasn't sure if I had permission to stop them. This was a new world. I had no husband.

I scanned the hall for Abram, but he was in a side room with Pharaoh, deep in conversation, seemingly unperturbed by the crowd around me. He was too far away. I stared at them, willing Abram to spot me and see my fear. Finally, Abram and Pharaoh looked directly at me. "Help," my eyes cried to his. "Let's go. Now." But though they were both staring at me, it was not my eyes but my body they examined. I watched as their gaze followed my hair, my skin, my breasts, waist, legs, feet.

I couldn't look at them any longer.

The table, the food - I would focus on that. I blocked out everyone who was looking at me. I stuffed some more quail into my mouth. I lifted the cup of wine to my lips and drained it.

Time passed. Dancers performed for us, and the music grew yet louder, and more dishes came. Then, out of the corner of my eye, I was aware of the parade of riches and goods that Pharaoh was bestowing on Abram - the grand show of cattle, donkeys, servants, gold. Abram had his head back, laughing, plainly giddy with relief that he was going to be rich rather than executed. He sneaked a 'thumbs up' smile at me; his plan had worked. Abram had sold me to Pharaoh. This was his payoff.

I tried to smile back, but my facial muscles would not obey me.

Food, food. I switched off my mind, focused on my stomach and took some more of the saffron rice. In the midst of the blur and noise of the richest party we had ever attended, I blocked it all out and kept eating, eating, eating.

***

By midnight, I was in my new quarters, the other wives and servants mingling and combing one another's hair while I lay huddled under my blanket, on the floor. I had been so hungry, but now my belly ached and stretched with the rich food, and I felt nauseous.

Whereas before my mind had been foggy, now it was terrifyingly clear, and I was acutely aware of my position. At any moment, my new master could claim me for his wife and sleep with me. Without Abram, I had no protector, no advocate.

I could not refuse him. The Pharaoh hadn't yet seen me naked, but I already felt violated. It was only a matter of time.

That's when the shame came like acid, so that I squirmed and writhed and curled up as small as I could under the covers. I wanted to make my body so small it would disappear.

Before that day, I had been secretly proud of my beauty. I may not have held a child in my arms, I may be looked down on by others, but my hair was long and shiny, my figure tall and curvy, and people stopped and noticed when I walked down the street. My beauty was an asset - perhaps my only asset - that kept me admired by others and adored by my husband.

That day, in a matter of hours, my beauty had turned from blessing to curse. I had been slobbered over by strangers and mentally undressed by the crowd while my husband looked on in approval. At some point when the main courses were served, I had ceased to be a person. I was just a bargaining chip, a prostitute to be offered up by my husband so we could get food. I wanted to crawl out of my own skin.

***

I clenched my fists around the blanket and tried to focus on its texture, away from the anxiety in my chest. The darkest thought formed at the back of my mind: perhaps it was solely Abram the Lord wanted to bless. Not me. Maybe I was the problem. In the early years, I had consciously pushed aside the question of whether Abram would have married me had he known I couldn't get pregnant. But now, at midnight, in a strange bed, I was defenceless against the doubts. I was a failed mother; a failed wife; a failed woman.

Those big promises of God's came back to mock me. I had thought the Lord's plan involved me, but perhaps this was the moment Abram would move on ahead of me and I would be written out of history.

I cried out to the Lord in piteous, wordless sobs. I didn't know what else to do.

At any moment the Pharaoh would come for me and force himself on me. (Would he? Would it be tonight?)

I couldn't stand the suspense. I just wanted it to be over already, or for me to be somewhere else. The silence and uncertainty were almost worse than the fate I faced. I wanted to leave my body and float far away. I dug my nails into my hands to distract myself from the agony of the wait, twitching at the slightest sound.

It was a long night.

***

The next day, I awoke, aching and sore, to the sound of vomiting. It wasn't just one of the girls who was sick; it was all of them. The room was saturated with the stench of sweat and stomach acid, and the women shivered with fever. This went on for several days.

As the sickness continued to spread amongst his harem, Pharaoh didn't ask for any of us, for fear of being infected, which was a relief for me. Meals were subdued affairs in the women's quarters in comparison with the first night, with people exiting abruptly from the table when their bowels betrayed them. It was hard to catch sight of Abram, who presumably was still somewhere in the palace, and I wondered if he had succumbed to this mysterious fever.

After a few more days, one of the servants told us that Pharaoh, spooked by the masses of people ill, had begun eating alone. When the boils started to appear, that's when Pharaoh got really alarmed. It seemed like almost everyone had come down with food poisoning, or some mysterious virus - apart from me and, as I later discovered, Abram. Yet we had all eaten the same food, so there was no reason we should be spared. It was starting to look suspicious, and some of the women were giving me dark looks and whispering rumours of poisoning.

It wasn't an unreasonable conclusion to reach. If I were the host, I would probably be suspecting foul play - we were newcomers, after all. I spent hours pacing around the grounds, avoiding everyone else, fanning myself to cool down from the oppressive heat, trying to distract myself from the fear. So far, no one had died, but no one had recovered. I was balancing in my mind which would be worse: to live for the rest of my life in a harem, die from this virus or be executed by Pharaoh on suspicion of poisoning. On the bad days, I wasn't sure which outcome I preferred.

At last, I was summoned to Pharaoh's great hall. I shot a glance at Abram, the only other person in the room, who looked as scared as I felt. I found myself shaking.

"What have you done to me?" Pharaoh bellowed.

We stood: frozen, silent.

The blood pounded in my ears, yet I found myself floating out of my body, as though I were looking down on myself. That had happened a few times to me since we had come to Egypt.

I felt utterly disconnected from my life, perfectly calm. Pharaoh was going to kill us. There would be no fame, no great nation, no permanent home for us, just a painful death at the hands of an angry Egyptian. It was as though I saw it clearly for the first time. I felt almost serene, though my body continued to shake.

Then came the most unexpected words from Pharaoh's lips, addressed to Abram: "Why didn't you tell me she was your wife?"

He sounded injured and bemused, not angry. There was no condemnation, no execution - nothing. If we were scared, Pharaoh was terrified. He realised he had sinned by taking someone's wife as his own, and he feared the Lord, who had the power to afflict him in this way. It wasn't a coincidence - the mysterious sickness had been a prod from God that something was amiss.

This foreigner - who had never known God - honoured God. Before we knew it, we were heading back home with everything we had, plus the dowry presents from Pharaoh.

***

The journey back was quiet. Abram was a little sheepish, though not apologetic, and, after his few attempts at jovial small-talk, we fell into silence. It would be a while until I could look him in the eye again. Something had broken in me in Egypt; perhaps it would never be fully repaired.

However, I was also quiet for another reason. The mysterious sickness; our mysterious health; Pharaoh's unexpected reaction: I had been saved, after all, and by supernatural means.

That horrible, horrible night when I had sobbed in desperation - the Lord had heard me. Perhaps it really was possible that the Lord hears us when no one else does. Now I was safely back with my husband, heading home, but this time with riches and plenty of food and servants.

That's what I thought during the whole journey back: the Lord heard me. The Lord had honoured me when my husband had not. I told myself then: the next time I feel humiliated, ignored, defeated, I will remember this feeling. Because in that moment, though everyone else had let me down, I knew I mattered to the Almighty.

To reflect on:

"But the Lord inflicted serious diseases on Pharaoh and his household because of Abram's wife Sarai."

Genesis 12:17

For further reading:

Genesis 12:10-20

Over to you:

1. Abram - called by God - feared for his life and did not trust that God would protect him; Pharaoh - a pagan - recognised God and feared him. What interests you about this contrast? Reflect on it for a while, and the ways that we see this pattern today.

2. "I mattered to the Almighty." Women were not valued highly in Abram's society, but God saw Sarai and honoured her. When have you experienced being honoured by God? How easy do you find it to remember that you matter to the Almighty? How can you remind yourself that you matter to Him?

3. "The Lord hears us when no one else does." Later in Genesis, Hagar calls God 'the God who sees' (Gen 16:13). Think of situations in your life that you long for God to hear or see. In your prayers today, remember the God who hears, the God who sees.

3. The Longing
Sarah's Story (Genesis 17:1-27)

When I waved goodbye to my sisters back in Harran, I thought that would be the hardest part. But it's not. You want to know the hardest part? It's the waiting.

I expected deep and short grief, but not this: the ongoing, relentless disappointment. We left, but we have never really landed anywhere. We just keep wandering. With all the potential enemies around who could try to throw us out, I feel on my guard all the time. We're in the land, we're settled; but it all feels so fragile, so temporary.

I am the world's most proficient packer. Ask anyone. I can dismantle a tent in under ten minutes, single-handedly. I can wrap our entire belongings in a few sheepskin bags without so much as breaking a sweat.

I've got good at it over the years; I've had to. I remember the shade of the great tree at Moreh, the pink flowers at Bethel, the hot summers in the Negev - and the brief excursion to the dark river of Egypt. After that the places blur into one - we just keep moving.

Sometimes I wish that God knew what it was like to be a wanderer with no place to call home. Maybe then he would understand what he has asked of us.

***

It's an unusually cold day today, the kind when you feel compelled to say, 'Isn't it cold?' every five minutes, because of the ongoing shock of the temperature. I rummage in the tent and wrap my blanket around myself for warmth. I remind myself that we have been in Mamre a while now, though I still don't feel like I belong. In many ways we're thriving, so I can see why outsiders congratulate us for being entrepreneurs who left home and made their fortune. You'd have trouble counting our sheep; we have quite the farm now, and I'm proud of managing our large team of workers. But those same outsiders note the lack of family, and you can see the questions on their lips.

In the distance, I can see Abram leaning against a fence, gesticulating and instructing our newest farm worker, whose face is pink with cold.

There is a chill in the air, and the clouds look thick with snow. I start calculating how much food we have in store, in case the snow is heavier than expected.

My bones ache, and my fingers are turning purple as I inspect the bags of grain.

I'm lonely.

Each year we get richer, and the farm grows, but I feel a little emptier.

We've been here for more than twenty years, but what do we have to show for it? A bit of land, more animals. No children in my arms. The other day, a friend pointed out that my posture is always hunched over because my default position is to fold my arms over my stomach. I hadn't realised. Even my arms are conscious of what should be there but isn't.

***

Every few years, I feel it, usually before Abram does: the doubt. Did we hear it right? Are we crazy? Have we displeased the Creator? Does he even exist? Then a few weeks later, out of nowhere, the Creator comes again. The Lord repeats those words that have grown faint and faded over time, and we have greater clarification.

Abram changes after these visits - I see his eyes light up again, his strength renewed. Of course, I only hear the promises via Abram, not the Creator Himself. Perhaps if I heard them from the Lord's lips, rather than Abram's, I would bounce back after a period of doubt, too. I envy Abram's friendship with the Creator, though I can never tell anyone that.

The other week, we were snapping at each other and the servants, separated from one another by our clouds of doubt. It got so bad that I made an excuse and went for a walk to the stream, so I could think. Part of me wanted to keep on walking until I got back to Harran. I stood by the stream and looked up at the sky.

"Will I ever bear a child? Am I even a part of your great plan?" I couldn't even say the words out loud, but this was what I wanted the Lord to answer. Stopping in my tracks, I waited for an answer, as tears ran down my cheeks. We were following the Lord's plan, yet it all felt so wrong. I needed something - reassurance, a miracle, a sign. I needed an end to the waiting.

No angel appeared, and the stream continued to gurgle and giggle.

I walked back home again.

***

Three days after that walk to the stream, Abram burst through the tent door with a huge grin on his face. Of course, I'm getting his name wrong - it's no longer Abram. That, in fact, was what he came to tell me. The Creator had appeared and repeated the promise - land, a great nation, a son, even a time-limit on how long we had to wait. Abraham was delighted. I should have been more grateful than I was. After all, the Lord had mentioned me specifically, not just Abraham, and said that I would bear a child.

But I was so tired of words. I had wanted action.

The name changes were so strange. Why change our names when they mean almost exactly the same as before? We're still ostensibly called 'father' and 'princess'. It seemed ridiculous at first.

Since then, I've seen why. It's not so much the meaning of the new names that's significant, it's that the Lord attached a promise to them. Abraham will be a father of many nations, I the mother of nations, and our descendants will be kings and rulers.

Abr-*ah*-am. Sar-*ah*. Every time I add that extra syllable to my husband's name or hear his new pronunciation of mine, it is an act of faith, minute by minute, acknowledging that the Creator spoke to us and called us. Even though we've spent decades wandering the countryside like vagrants, each time we call to one another it is a reminder to us that God has spoken, and we carry the promise of land and children.

The new names baffle our friends and family. After all, if you're going to make a change, why not a proper change?

That's what I feel: there is a change, but barely. Sometimes I feel a renewed sense of hope in God's promise - but it quickly fades. More than a joy, it is a discipline to keep repeating the names God gave us, because it comes with a call to trust. Again. Again.

My teeth are chattering. I move the grain bags back into place and sigh.

How long can one person carry on believing, when the reality bears no resemblance to the promise? When we left Harran, Abr-ah-am was already seventy-five. It was already a long-shot for us to have children, and now it has been another twenty-four years. Twenty-four years! Would you think that a reasonable delay? It is a long, long time to believe nice words in the face of the overwhelming evidence to the contrary.

For 8760 days I have been walking this tightrope of hope and disappointment, and I don't know if I can walk it much longer. That day by the stream, what I really craved from the Creator was action, not words.

I wanted fulfilment; instead, God repeated the promise.

I cling to the words, but sometimes I feel as if my whole life has been a long wandering, a long hunger that hasn't yet been satisfied.

To reflect on:

"God also said to Abraham, "As for Sarai your wife, you are no longer
to call her Sarai; her name will be Sarah. I will bless her and will
surely give you a son by her. I will bless her so that she will be the
mother of nations; kings of peoples will come from her.""

Genesis 17:15-16

For further reading:

Genesis 17:1-27

Over to you:

1. "I feel as if my whole life has been a long wandering, a long hunger
    that hasn't yet been satisfied." To what extent can you relate to this?
    To what degree does this describe the Christian experience?

2. "Sometimes I wish that God knew what it was like to be a wanderer
    with no place to call home." Jesus later described himself, saying
    'Foxes have dens and birds have nests, but the Son of Man has no
    place to lay his head' (Luke 9:58). John describes Jesus' incarnation
    in this way: 'And the word became flesh and lived among us' (John
    1:14). Literally it translates as, 'pitched his tent among us'. When
    you are feeling lost and rootless, what difference does it make to
    meditate on these verses?

3. "I wanted fulfilment: instead, God repeated the promise." When
    have you found this to be true for you? Which promises of God -
    either from the Bible or more specifically for your life - do you need
    to hear repeatedly?

4. "It is an act of faith, minute by minute, acknowledging that the
    Creator spoke to us and called us." What daily reminders do you
    have that God has spoken to you, called you, given you promises?
    If you don't have those daily reminders, what could you make or
    use that would help you remember?

4. The Visitors
Sarah's Story (Genesis 18:1-15)

It was hot that day in the tent, no breeze at all. By midday I was sweating profusely, and I felt a little queasy. Pausing from my work, I lifted the smaller jar and poured myself some water. From my position in the centre of the tent, I could see Abraham sitting at the entrance, humming to himself, lost in his thoughts. Beyond him was our land; the goat pens; the fields; the cluster of trees. Then, suddenly: three men.

I spotted them before Abraham did, and I immediately wondered why our scouts hadn't seen them and checked them for weapons. That would be the prudent thing to do - we were a rich community now, with plenty of assets, and there were always those who came to look for weaknesses to exploit. Screwing up my eyes, I tried to read their faces, but I couldn't make them out. Possibly they were just looking for shade. It was so hot. I remembered my water and sipped slowly.

I ought to be alerting Abraham or springing into action - whether to welcome them or fight them, I still wasn't sure. Still, I stayed where I was, sipping the water. My queasiness grew, and whether it was the sunshine or something supernatural I will never know, but their faces seemed both lit-up and obscure; shimmering, perhaps, in the heat. I took a final swig of water and placed the cracked cup down.

Finally Abraham noticed them, a good few minutes after me. Naturally, my husband, always one to make friends with potential enemies, ran with his arms outstretched. I stayed in the tent, hiding behind the tent flaps like a child.

When Abraham ran back, buzzing with excitement about possible messengers from the Lord, part of me wasn't surprised. I had felt it in my blood. Of course, I ought to have been excited, like Abraham, but I couldn't summon the emotional energy. He flapped at me with great joy and gave me recipe orders, as if I needed to be instructed to use the finest flour. But I was weary and unsettled, so I just nodded mutely.

Abraham ran back to the shade of the big oak tree, and I was left alone. I got the best flour out, like a good wife, and began making the bread. I cupped the flour together in my hands as I had done so many times before and made a well with my finger. I stared at the empty hole.

***

Because I had grown up in a big family, surrounded by fun and a noisy variety of people, I had always imagined we would have a big family, too.

I could cope with four, I reasoned. When the Lord's promise came, I had to recalculate - seven, twelve, twenty would be more of a challenge, but I was ready for it all; ready to be this great family, a new nation, just as God had promised us.

I poured the water into the well and collapsed the flour around it.

I thought of the early days of marriage, before the great promise. All I had ever wanted to do was nurture a child, shape another life. Today, a little nauseous from the heat, I remembered all those days when I had been thrilled at the slightest feeling of nausea. I had longed for a sign that new life had begun inside me. My sisters, cousins, friends, everyone - I listened to their stories and took mental notes. They all got pregnant, one after another, and I waited for my story to follow. But it didn't.

I smacked the flour and water together, forcing them to combine into dough, grinding my hand against the surface of the wood.

Hearing God's promise reignited my hope. Each month, I had bled, and each month I told myself not to be disappointed: it would happen next month. The months went on, and I wondered if we had heard right. My thoughts followed the same loop over and over: maybe Abraham is mistaken; maybe it's my fault; maybe the Lord has forgotten; maybe the Lord is punishing me. I prayed desperate prayers of blanket repentance over and over, thinking of every small thing that the Lord might possibly be holding against me. I had scourged myself with blame and shame.

I picked up the dough in my hands, stretching it out, squashing it back together. I picked it up again. I toyed with it, watching idly while it stretched to breaking point. Then I slapped it back together again and went on playing with it.

***

Of course, after a while, everyone had an explanation for why it hadn't happened. They gave me potions; taught bizarre techniques; told me to abandon 'this old-fashioned creator-god' and worship the fertility gods, as any normal person would do.

I clung to hope for a good few years after marriage, before it faded into resignation. When God first promised Abraham a big family, my hope reignited; the rush of longings I'd submerged returned in full force. The first month passed and ended in blood. The second month, the third, the fourteenth, the thirtieth - they all passed the same way.

In the midst of the aching lack of a child, I couldn't have anticipated losing friends, too. One friend told me - to my face - because I didn't worship the fertility god that secretly meant I despised children and was glad not to be a mother, deserving no sympathy. Another friend approached Abraham directly, telling him to leave me: he could start again with a better breeder. I had played Hide and Seek with these women in my childhood, cheered them on at their weddings, held their first baby in my arms. I never spoke to them again.

I got mad at God.

Years passed.

I stopped being mad at God, simply because I hadn't the energy for it any longer. Every month, we had the relentless rhythm of hope, disappointment; hope, disappointment; hope, disappointment.

I flung the dough onto the board and leaned my whole weight into the kneading action. The wood hurt my fist as I worked, but I pressed harder still.

***

There's only so long you can hope before it breaks you. I disciplined myself to stop thinking about it. Some part of me shut down. Gradually, I began to accept that it was not to me that the Lord had promised a child. We'd misunderstood. Perhaps the Lord had wanted us to take action; anything was better than waiting.

I couldn't face a single extra year of being stuck in limbo, so I decided to find a solution. When you have been driven mad by waiting, you will do anything - even things you previously thought abhorrent - just to end the stalemate.

Honestly, I thought I would be okay with my servant having my husband's baby. I told myself it was like ordering something you wanted; I was still in control. She would be my surrogate. I could be a mother.

But then - *her* - the look on her face when she had the very thing I had longed for, and Abraham looking so proud, so pleased, so unbearably paternal - I couldn't stand it. I didn't want her baby, this usurper. My loss became a jagged metal spike that pierced my inner organs. I had no idea I could hate so fiercely.

Every time she held that child in her arms, I thought of the child that should be in my arms, the child I was promised. The Lord God had lied to me.

***

The smell of wood-smoke and roasting veal drifted into the tent; our servant had worked fast. My bread ought to have been proving by now, of course.

I pounded the dough, squashing out all the air from it, beads of sweat forming on my forehead as I worked. When I paused, my knuckles throbbing with pain, I heard a voice from over by the trees. One of the Lord's messengers was saying, "Oh, but Sarah will have a baby next year." There was once a time when a comment like that would have floored me and left me reeling for days, sobbing and crying at the broken promises. But I was beyond that now.

I wanted to say to the Lord's messenger, "You have a pretty sick sense of humour. It has been too long. It's over. You can't just keep promising things when we both know it is never going to happen. Stop lying to me."

Standing there, hidden in the tent, in the sweltering heat, flour on my hands, I felt a white rage pushing up in my chest. It came out of my throat as laughter.

I laughed, but I wanted to punch someone. I laughed like a threatened lion roars.

They were too far away to hear me, or so I thought, but the messengers turned around to stare at me. I swallowed it all down again, kept my eyes focused on my hands, and I went on pounding the bread as though nothing had happened.

One of them beckoned me over. Taking a deep breath, I wiped the flour off my hands, walked to the tree and stood before him, defiant.

There was something about his demeanour that reminded me of my mother. His eyes held gentleness, power and deep love. In his presence, my anger gave way to discomfort, and I had a peculiar sense of being utterly known. In Egypt, I had been mentally undressed by men, but here was someone who saw past my body through to my soul. I clasped my hands together tightly to keep all the emotion in, my nails digging into my skin.

The Messenger gave me the smallest of smiles, then turned to Abraham.

"Why did Sarah laugh? Is anything too hard for the Lord?"

I blinked back tears.

He knew me. He knew what I was thinking. I had nowhere to hide. It was like staring into the face of the God who had formed my body, and I wanted a fig leaf or two to cover me.

And then the thought came to me, "What if it really is happening this time?" Just minutes before, I had been furious with God, resenting Him, quietly defying Him. But maybe the Lord was actually on the point of giving us a baby. He had seen my inner thoughts. What if now I had ruined it, all because I couldn't wait any longer and laughed?

I was suddenly afraid, where I hadn't been afraid before. So I lied.

"No, I didn't laugh," I said. I said it with as much bravado as I could muster, because he had transformed this old lady into an eight-year-old girl again, stealing raisin cakes from my mother.

"Yes, you did laugh," he said. I saw love in his eyes, and I wanted to weep.

To reflect on:

"Then the Lord said to Abraham, "Why did Sarah laugh and say, 'Will I really have a child, now that I am old?' Is anything too hard for the Lord? I will return to you at the appointed time next year, and Sarah will have a son.""

Genesis 18:13-14

For further reading:

Genesis 18:1-15

Over to you:

1. Have you ever felt like Sarah, like God has a sick sense of humour and you can't wait any longer?

2. "I laughed." "I lied." When has your reaction to a difficult situation been like Sarah's?

3. "Is anything too hard for the Lord?" What do you find encouraging about this biblical phrase as you wait? What challenges you?

5. The Laughter
Sarah's Story (Genesis 21:1-7)

I always thought I would enjoy being pregnant. After all, I had longed for it all my life, watched with envy as other women's bodies blossomed with new life. But now that it was here - so late, so strangely - I didn't know how to respond. My sleep turned into a long series of nightmares where I gave birth to a vicious, thrashing snake, as blood covered my body. I kept waking in the night, sweating; my heart beating fast and the baby furiously kicking my stomach. I couldn't shake the image from my mind.

When you have been disappointed for so long, it is hard to trust. I wanted to hope that everything would be okay. After all, this was the miracle pregnancy that had got everyone buzzing. Our little community had become very crowded as news spread. Strangers wanted to see me and stare, or - worse - touch my stomach. Some came with pain in their eyes, hoping for my miraculous fertility to rub off on them and relieve them of their childlessness. Those I found harder to turn away.

While others glowed in pregnancy, I felt sick and tired. I grew breathless from walking the smallest amount, and Abraham hovered around me, asking if there was anything I needed, and whether I wouldn't want to lie down.

Finally, with the support of my female friends, I rested for the end of the pregnancy. I talked to them about the birth. They were all supportive, but I knew the risks. I'd seen for myself the deaths of women in childbirth, and the older you got, the riskier it was. Everything felt so precarious, so improbable.

"But of course it's improbable, it's the Lord's doing! He is the creator of life!" Abraham would say with excitement. "Look at the timing - less than a year after the Lord visited us in Mamre! All God's promises are coming true."

Desperately, I tried to replace the image of the nightmares in my mind with the memory of the Lord's promise at Mamre. I wanted to believe him. I also wanted - as always - to be sure we had heard right this time. My heart was already bruised, and I wanted to protect it from being broken.

***

Labour was slow and painful - much slower than most of the other childbirths I'd seen. My ageing body was being pushed to its limits, I knew, and I dared not even shout in pain, as though I were anticipating more pain yet to come. In our tent, the midwives encircled me as I pushed in silence. Time blurred, and it felt like I would always be in that position, pushing for the rest of my life.

Whenever I felt myself getting panicky with the pain, I looked up at the tent, where there was a circle of light above me. At one point I saw an angel there - like the Messengers at Mamre, but with wings; although, I was fairly delirious by that stage, so I was never completely sure whether it was real. I like to think it was.

"The baby's head is crowning," the midwife said to me. "One final push - you can do it."

I pushed, finally letting myself utter a single guttural groan. The volume of it surprised me, but I kept my eyes upon that circle of light above me: breathing out, panting, gasping, but always looking up.

"The baby's out," the midwives announced, but they said nothing afterwards, and the tent was ominously silent. It was too quiet - something was wrong. After all this time, had the baby died, after all?

Just when I thought the worst, a cry pierced the air. Normally a baby's cry is an ugly sound, but at that moment it was utterly beautiful, the start of a song.

Before, if you had asked me what emotion I would express at the birth of my baby, I would have said for sure that I would be in tears at the relief and beauty of it, but that's not what happened. At the moment of his scream, pure joy swelled inside me, and I burst into laughter.

He cried; I laughed.

They brought him to me, red and angry-faced, and I held him close. He was healthy; tiny but feisty. His cry and my giggles intermingled, and soon the midwives were laughing, too, at the sheer foolishness and ridiculousness of it all.

"God has brought me laughter, and everyone who hears about this will laugh with me," I said. Then with a jolt, I remembered something that Abraham had said: the Lord had promised I would have a baby, and we would call him Isaac, 'he laughs'.

This was the Lord's doing. That was the moment when something shifted in me, and I believed. At that moment, I was so full of joy it was almost painful - my chest couldn't contain it. This was the overwhelming, life-giving joy of the Lord.

I stroked my baby's head and whispered so that only he and the Lord would hear, "You will be a great nation. You will bless all peoples."

That was the promise I had so often doubted, but now I handed it to my new son as a secret and precious gift. It had taken twenty-five years for God to fulfil his promise. It was such a long time to wait for something.

A thought suddenly occurred to me: when I had been impatient and despairing all those twenty-five years, what had God been feeling? Was it possible that God had been longing for this moment as much as me?

I looked down. My hands were wrinkled, covered in sun-spots and purple veins, yet they were filled with the soft skin of the baby. My baby. My empty hands were full at last, and all I could do was laugh. Perhaps God, also, was laughing with me.

To reflect on:

"Sarah said, "God has brought me laughter, and everyone who hears about this will laugh with me.""

Genesis 21:6

For further reading:

Genesis 21:1-7

Over to you:

"Had God been longing for this moment as much as me?" Sarah's story is about the redemption of laughter: from a laugh of bitter disappointment of waiting in limbo (Genesis 18:12) to a laugh of joy when God's promises came true (Genesis 21:6). God proved to be faithful to his promises, but it was also a very, very long time before it happened. For us, some of God's promises take longer than we expect. For some of us, there are promises we won't fully experience this side of heaven.

1. "God has brought me laughter." How does your heart respond when you hear those words? To what extent has this been true in your life?

2. When you next laugh, pay attention to it. How is your laugh at the moment: is it tinged with bitterness or sadness, or is it pure joy? Without knowing whether your story will be a 'happy ending' this side of heaven, is there a possibility that your laughter can still contain joy rather than bitterness? What would it take for this to happen?

6. General Reflections
Sarah's Story

As you look back through Sarah's story:

1. Which parts came to life for you in a new way?

2. Which parts most resonated with your experience?

3. Which parts challenged, troubled or encouraged you?

4. Which aspects of God's character did you glimpse in Sarah's story?

5. Which verses would you want to memorise or meditate on further?

6. We often want a clear reason for God delaying good things. We want to know the reason why. Sarah's story doesn't give us a clear reason. Instead, Sarah's life tells us that:

   a) we should follow the guidance God is giving us, even though it looks strange;
   b) God has not forgotten us;
   c) God honours us;
   d) God wants us to trust again;
   e) God longs to bring us joy.

As you think about your own journey with waiting, or supporting others in theirs, which of these truths about God do you need to remember or share?

Some of these reflections and exercises are repeated in the Group Bible Study.

Creative Exercise: Name changes

God changed Abram and Sarai's names, just subtly, to encourage their spirits so that they would pause and remember God.

If you could imagine God changing your name through this process of conscious waiting, what name would you hope God gave you? (You might use a baby name book, or a website where you can search for the meaning and find a name, e.g. Behindthename.com/search.php.) Write that new name on a stone and keep it as a reminder of hope.

Creative Exercise: Love letter from God

After you have looked back through the last year, consider writing an affirming love letter to yourself, as though it were God writing to you. What does he think about you? What does he want to say to you about this year? What does he want you to remember?

This is what I imagine such a love letter might look like if God were writing to Sarah:

Dear Sarah,

I know you think I've forgotten you and that I don't see you, I just see <u>Abraham</u>. The truth is I love you and value you very much. Remember the time <u>in Egypt</u>, when <u>Abraham behaved so appallingly?</u> I was angry that <u>he dishonoured you and abandoned you.</u>

I want you to know that I will never do that to you. I am here for you. I know it's hard for you to trust me right now, because <u>it's been so many years and you still haven't had a baby.</u> I know it's your heart's desire, and how unbearable it is for you to wait. I know you thought that it would solve things <u>for Hagar to have a baby,</u> and it hasn't; it's made it worse. I know all this, and I love you through it all.

I'm asking you to wait a little longer. I know it's tough, but I'm hoping you can find me in the waiting. I'm here, and I love you very much. You are so precious to me, and I delight in you. I see you, even when so many others don't. Keep going.

With much love, God

What would your love letter from God say? Take some time, go to a place where you feel comfortable and have minimal distraction, and write that letter as though you were writing from God to you. If you need a template, replace the underlined parts with your experience. How does it feel to write it?

Music

Take some time this week to listen to an advent hymn about waiting for Jesus, e.g. Come, Thou Long Expected Jesus (Charles Wesley); Joy to the World, the Lord is Come (Isaac Watts); Lo, He Comes with Clouds Descending (Charles Wesley).

Pray

God loves Abrahams and Sarahs equally, and we need each other. Pray for and encourage one another in our different situations, remembering God's grace to all.

Heart-cry Prayer

Lord, it has been too long. You never show up - and then you come at the worst time possible, and I am not ready to speak to you. I don't know if I want to trust you again. I don't know if I can. Please be gentle. Please be kind. That's all I've got. Amen.

Benediction for Sarahs

May you who are cloaked in and choked by cynicism
Be broken by the grace of God.

May you who are in hiding
Find God's hands held out to you
As an open invitation of love.

May you see God's face when it all feels too late,
And may you encounter God,
Who sees you, knows you, loves you still. Amen.

Benediction for Abrahams

May you who have been hoping long
Be sustained in that hope.

May you who keep your heart as an open place
Be cherished, not bruised;

And may the God of hope lighten your spirit,
As you lighten the spirits of others. Amen.

SECTION TWO
Isaiah's Story

Dealing with Delay
Waiting for Justice and Peace

Prelude to Isaiah's Story

From Sarah and Abraham, roll the clock forward. Their progeny bloomed into twelve tribes who toiled as slaves in Egypt. They escaped, walking through the Red Sea into the wilderness. Then out they spread, into the fertile land Abraham had always been searching for: Canaan.

Swords flashed and blood spilt as Abraham's descendants fought great nations for the land. They were rescued time after time by God, whenever they remembered they were supposed to worship the Lord and cry to him for help. Slowly, Abraham's people filled the land.

Flick forward the calendar pages again: 1000 years after Sarah lived. Twelve tribes melded into one nation, united under a king, under God. Great King David built his palace in Jerusalem, establishing it as the capital, leaving his son, Solomon, to build the temple. There God would dwell with them. It seemed nothing could stop this united nation - until it split.

Only a generation after Solomon, the great marriage became a great divorce, as Solomon's son ruled Jerusalem and the South, and an upstart army general took the northern land and most of the people with him. The two mini-nations, weakened by the split, were called Judah in the south and Israel in the north.

Spin the clock hands again for another 250 years, when revolutions and wars rocked both nations, especially Israel. It is now the eighth century BC.

Zoom in on Jerusalem, in the small nation of Judah. It is now a great and revered city with strong walls, protected by the presence of God in its temple. As you look over this historic city you spot a single man walking upright amidst the crowds: a worshipper of the Lord who could trace his family tree back to Sarah. His name is Isaiah.

1. How Long, O Lord?
Isaiah's Story (Isaiah 6:1-13)

You never know the day that will change your life.

I awoke early, turning in my bed while it was still dark, watching the slow lightening of the sky till I could get up without disturbing the family.

I had always vowed to stay away from politics. Now I feared I had been complacent, perhaps even naive. Peeling myself off the floor, I crept out of the house, hoping a short walk would stop my increasing anxiety.

***

King Uzziah was dying. It wasn't official, of course. His people had been putting out the message that he was still in control, as all loyal advisors should, even as behind closed doors his skin disintegrated, prefiguring the destruction of his inner organs. He had managed to linger on longer than expected, but his days were numbered; of that I was sure.

The sun had not yet fully risen. Morning mist dampened the air as I set out towards the centre of Jerusalem, though it would be warm by the afternoon. I heard Uzziah's name carried on the breeze. In huddles, the early-rising city-folk were already gossiping, twitching and glancing behind themselves as they spoke, lest people should interpret it as wishing the king dead. Their faces betrayed their morbid excitement. As I turned the corner, I spotted the royal baker, surrounded by a clutch of locals clamouring to know the latest news. He nodded at me as I passed.

The walk was not working. I sighed. There was no way I could distract myself from politics. Giving in, I allowed my brain to whir while my feet pounded.

It was impossible to imagine life without Uzziah on the throne. A good king with peace in the land is like your parent's furniture: you don't notice it till it's gone. He had been reigning since before I was born. Now he was fading, and at the worst time possible. Out of nowhere, in quiet Assyria, a warrior with a thirst for blood had gained control of the kingdom. Unconquerable, and greedy for power and land, Tiglath-Pileser III was on the move, and our priests and prophets were worried.

As I made my way through the streets, the mist heightened the odours of the city. Jerusalem could smell wonderful: roasted meat in the distance from the temple; morning bread baking; herbs and crushed flowers for medicine; but today, it stank of urine, blood and faeces, both human and animal. My nose scented the group of women before I saw them: at the end of another narrow street they were laughing and chatting as they scaled fish together. Fish-blood and purple guts pooled at their feet. I wondered if they, too, were concerned about Assyria. But they gutted their fish quite cheerfully.

***

I took a shortcut to avoid the stench. Down the alleyway I saw two young brothers; one had the other in a chokehold. Immediately their mother ran out from a dark corner and physically separated them while they both screamed.

It's family fights that are the most bitter, even in politics. Once our brother-nation, I no longer trusted Israel in the north to be our allies in a war. They could turn on us at any time. Even now they could be plotting with another country - Syria, perhaps - to declare war on us.

Only now were we realising our good fortune of living without warfare for decades. What an outrageous privilege it is to live in peace. How had I not been more aware of it before?

My perspiration intermingled with the mist, and I could feel the burn on the back of my calves as I pushed upwards, upwards, upwards. I emerged from the alleyway, blinked a little at the light, and paused to admire the roofs on either side of me: temple and palace, God and King, both holding our country together.

We had been blessed, but what would happen once Uzziah died? We were a small nation. The court had done their best to contain the rumours, but now all of Jerusalem could smell the threat.

Where was God in all of this? My feet were moving of their own accord as I entered the first court, and I realised this was the question in my heart as I reached the temple doorway. Where was God? I had wandered to the temple, half asleep, because I had wanted to meet God.

I had no idea what that would actually mean.

***

People tell me, even today, "You saw God and lived! I wish it could have been me!"

I laugh at them, because they have no idea what they are asking.

I was terrified. That's what I remember: the fear. When I say angels and light, it wasn't exactly moon-glow: my eyes were burning.

Angels are fireballs with wings. Still want to meet an angel?

When the angels sang, I felt no inner peace, no glorious soothing music for my soul. They were loud - literally earth-shatteringly loud. The walls vibrated with the sound; the ground below and doorway above me started shaking, and I thought the whole temple would collapse on my head. Even as I tried to regain my balance, there was smoke everywhere, and I coughed and spluttered. Every single second, I thought of a different way I would die.

What did God look like? This is the question whispered to me by curious children warned not to make graven images. I couldn't tell you even now. I saw God, but I can only describe to you the hem of his robe, the throne he was sitting on. That's all my brain could hold. The richness of God was too much for me.

The temple, the world, my being - everything was full of God in that moment, and my skin could not contain all that I was experiencing. It was wonderful - which is to say, I was full of wonder but shaken to my core.

***

I had seen God. Naturally, I was convinced I would die, right there in the temple. I couldn't tear my eyes away from his glory. It made me feel more alive, more whole, than I had ever been before; yet at the same time, the unbearable purity of God's light left me hoping the ground would swallow me up.

You have to know - this is not my usual way of being. Generally, I think I am a pretty good specimen of God's handiwork. I am proud of the work I do and the person I am. I'm not arrogant - not really - just blessed with an inner confidence. It took me five years to discover that I'd mortally offended cousin Jehiel. I operate on the premise that people are pleased with me, unless they tell me otherwise.

In that moment, however, I was destroyed.

I wanted to explode myself and start again. When I saw the pure brilliance of God, my eyes were opened to my sin: all the times I had been selfish or cruel; all the ways I had closed my heart to the needs of others; all my complacent apathy when I had witnessed others' suffering. A lifetime of sin dropped on my soul in that moment, like dung. It's not that

I wanted to die when I saw God; it was more like some inner part of me did die, and I was convinced that my physical death would soon follow.

***

That's when the fiery angel flew to get a burning coal from the altar: red-hot and coming straight for me. I closed my eyes in terror as the rock grew closer, steeling myself for the pain and the end of my life.

My eyes were still closed when the coal touched my lips, but there was no pain. I blinked open my eyes in surprise and heard the words, "See... your guilt is taken away and your sin atoned for".

Instead of pain, I'd received forgiveness.

Instead of death, I experienced resurrection.

I looked up and saw light, holiness, an overwhelming sense of goodness. What broke me the most was the Lord's love. It was the kind of love that makes you simultaneously want to laugh with joy and cry with shame, like breaking a family heirloom and being fully embraced and held anyway.

Then the Lord himself spoke, his words simultaneously thunderously loud and a gentle invitation:

"Whom shall I send? And who will go for us?"

I said the only thing I could have said to God in the circumstances, "Here am I. Send me."

Rather than condemnation, I'd received a commission.

A strange commission it was, too. Knock the people out of their complacency, tell them of the need to come back to God: this much I already understood, as I clutched the walls, trembling in the temple at the sheer beauty of God's presence. This was my story - from complacency to awe and repentance. I hoped for it to become the nation's story.

What I found harder to understand was God's warning to me that they would not listen.

"For how long, Lord?" I asked. What would it take for the country to wake up to danger, to return to God?

The answer was even more depressing: "Until the cities lie ruined."

God's people would refuse to listen to God until the country had been almost entirely obliterated. Only then would we see the smallest hope emerge.

***

In a daze, I stumbled back home, trying to process it all.

I was to be a prophet - but a prophet doomed to have his words ignored. No one would listen to me. The people would stay complacent and march on towards their ruin. I would be an unwilling witness to the almost-destruction of a land and people I loved deeply. I felt frustrated already: voiceless, helpless.

It was then that I stopped in my tracks, as the thought hit me.

Is that what God feels, too, when people don't listen?

***

It's all about perspective. Sometimes I still feel smothered by the worries of what will happen to our country as we stumble from one mistake to another. I still worry about what will happen to us, to my children, to the next generation. But right then, that day in the temple, I knew the smallness of the kings of this world, because I had seen something of the immensity of God.

To reflect on:

"And they were calling to one another: 'Holy, holy, holy is the Lord Almighty; the whole earth is full of his glory.'"

Isaiah 6:3

For further reading:

Isaiah 6:1-13

Note:

Isaiah's commission is puzzling: why would God give Isaiah a message then prevent the people from being able to respond to it? For those who struggle with verse 10 it is worth noting that Paul had a different interpretation of Isaiah's words, saying that God foreknew their stubbornness rather than foreordaining it:

"Go to this people and say, 'You will be ever hearing but never understanding
You will be ever seeing but never perceiving.
For this people's heart has become calloused;
they hardly hear with their ears,
and they have closed their eyes.
Otherwise they might see with their eyes,

> hear with their ears,
> understand with their hearts
> and turn, and I would heal them.' "(Acts 28:25-27)

It's therefore equally reasonable to read it as God predicting the inevitability of the people's refusal to listen to Isaiah rather than God actively willing their refusal to listen.

Over to you:

1. "The hem of his robe filled the temple" (Isaiah 6:1, NRSV). To what extent do you find the 'bigness' of God a comfort? How does it alter our perspective to consider God as a king or queen on the throne?

2. "Is that what God feels, too, when people don't listen?" Isaiah 6 challenges us both to a) listen to God's words more and b) live courageously and speak God's truth, even when people refuse to hear it. Which of those do you most need to take to heart today?

3. "For how long, Lord?" (Isaiah 6:11). So often that is the cry of our hearts when we are in a season of waiting. Isaiah waited his whole life for people to listen to his prophecies, and though he saw some of them fulfilled, he rarely saw people respond as they should to his prophecies. Isaiah and the psalmists all ask 'How long, O Lord?' It's not just an intellectual enquiry of God; it's often a prayer of desperation. Use some of David's words from Psalm 6 as a basis for prayer, or simply pray: 'How long, O Lord?'

2. The Short Wait for Immanuel
Isaiah's Story (Isaiah 7:1-25)

"This is it," I thought. "This will be the moment when my words will rescue a nation."

It was good news I was delivering to Ahaz, I repeated to myself, as I walked out of Jerusalem's gates with my son. We were walking along the ridge, towards the valley, to meet with the king. The view from Jerusalem that day was wondrous, and we could see the land of Judah at our feet. It was almost a decade since the Lord had called me to be a prophet, a decade since the temple shook and I'd trembled. King Uzziah's successor had already died, and now we were stuck with King Ahaz.

Ahead of me, Shear-Jashub gave a cry, and my heart thudded as he tripped over a stone and tumbled dangerously close to the edge of the ridge. I ran over to help him up. Whether he needed me or not, I couldn't stop my instinct to help him.

My wife had died in childbirth. For the past ten years, it had been just the two of us, and we'd clung to each other in the face of loss. I spotted tears in his eyes when he saw the blood, but he was a big boy now, determined to be brave. Already he was pushing my hands away and picking the little stones out of the cut on his knee. He was growing up so fast.

Suddenly, a memory: it was me who was his height, it was me on my hands and knees, embarrassed and bruised. I was with my father, who was at the palace on official business, but distracted by the palace art, I had tripped on a step, and my body slapped to the floor. At once, he had been there, kneeling beside me, helping me up, just as I had done with Shear-Jashub. I had dismissed his hands, just as Shear-Jashub had done with me. My father had delivered a stinging rebuke to the king that day, his face resolute even as the palace officials rolled their eyes, and a bold thrill had run through me as he spoke.

I had witnessed my father speaking truth to priests and kings. I had watched him being summarily dismissed as a result. This was potentially good training for my future-calling as a prophet, I thought wryly.

But I had better hopes for this particular message - perhaps my son would witness me making a difference. Was this why God had asked me to bring Shear-Jashub with me today?

***

We walked together, father and son, as I thought about our nation. As a small country, our security was already shaky, but since Ahaz had come to the throne, the enemy was at our gate. When I visited the baker yesterday, they had already run out of barley flour because everyone had been panic-buying. The whispers had spread and the rumours sounded true: in an act of betrayal, Ephraim - which is to say, Israel, once our brothers and compatriots - had formed an alliance with Syria against us.

It could be any day, so they were saying. Instinctively, I glanced over to the far hills, towards Syria. Sure enough, if you strained your eyes, you could spot scouts running here and there with clusters of soldiers behind them.

What was the solution to the crisis? In Jerusalem, the gossips were already suggesting the strategy King Ahaz must be considering: we should sign an alliance with the new bully in town, Assyria, so we could protect our land.

Shear-Jashub and I had reached the end of the ridge. There was now a winding path down to the valley, and I spotted the king and his entourage below. They looked so small from up here.

I seemed to be the sole voice counselling people to postpone the panic. Ephraim and Syria? I knew in my soul: they were no threat. They were already finished as superpowers. More than this, though, the people were afraid of the wrong enemy. God had warned me that Assyria was the nation we needed to beware, not Syria or Ephraim. A treaty with Assyria would be a disaster - perhaps *the* disaster of our generation.

We now descended into the valley, picking our way over stray stones on the path. A fly buzzed in my ear, and I flinched and flicked it away.

I was sure I could persuade the King to wait a little longer, to hold off signing anything for the next few months. God would come through for us.

It was good news we were delivering, I told my son, as we looked down over the trees below into the valley and continued our descent. But out of nowhere, a raven flew low, right in front of us, cawing mockingly, and without thinking, I found myself pulling my son tightly to me. The moment passed, and I told myself I was just being superstitious.

All the same, though, I remembered what the Lord had told us to call our son: Shear-Jashub, 'a remnant will return'. Why had God commanded me to bring him here today? Maybe it was so my boy could be a witness to my prophecy for the next generation, just as I had been a witness for my father's words. Perhaps this one meeting would be significant for our nation, our history.

As we walked alongside the aqueduct, we heard the distinctive buzz of soldiers gathering to fight. It was our own army.

The general recognised me and let me through begrudgingly. He saw me as a war detractor, a traitor who devalued men's sacrifice by questioning the military policy of the defence committee.

But I knew I was right.

While she was still alive, I had ranted to my wife, "It would save a lot of time if people could just agree with me in the first place." She would smile at me. But this time it was true, because I had heard God's Spirit. However nervous I felt approaching the king, I knew in my bones I was right.

***

It was dark and damp in the valley and the flies were out in force. Three army commanders holding a chart and nodding about numbers surrounded King Ahaz. He looked distracted in their midst as we marched up to him.

I put one hand on Shear-Jashub's shoulder and took a deep breath to deliver my speech.

"King Ahaz, you don't need to worry about Damascus and Ephraim defeating us. I know what everyone's saying - that they will conquer and annexe Judah. What happened in Elath, where people had to run for their lives from Syria's armies - that was bad, but don't let it influence you."

I tried to meet his gaze, but he seemed to be very busy with a map.

"I'm here to tell you not to be afraid. It's not going to happen. These nations are but smouldering wood - all burnt and finished. Their time is already up."

King Ahaz raised one eyebrow at me then looked pointedly across the valley, where small groups of soldiers were swarming on the other side.

Irritated, I swiped at the flies hovering around my face and tried again.

"If you do not stand firm in your faith, you will not stand at all."

I wanted him to see with spiritual eyes, to have the courage to wait a little longer. He needed to trust God and as a nation, we needed that, too. He walked towards another official, who handed him a chart, and he glanced up at the sun to check the time.

This was not going well.

I listened to the fiery voice in my soul and walked after him with fresh words.

"Ask the Lord your God for a sign," I pleaded. Perhaps he would believe on account of the sign, just as Gideon once had. Gideon had had no faith, convinced he would lose the battle, but after his rigmarole of putting out a fleece twice he finally believed. Maybe a sign was what Ahaz needed.

Ahaz glanced sideways at me and would not catch my eye.

"I will not ask; I will not put the Lord to the test," he said.

I stared at him awhile. He was looking firmly at the chart and examining the numbers, but I saw his neck and face turn scarlet.

'He's already done it,' I thought. I knew it in that moment. I knew it from his evasive manner, his hardened eyes. He had already signed a treaty with Assyria. He had already put his signature to our doom.

This is what we do when we fear. This is what we do when we feel we have been waiting for God for too long. We make treaties. We sign away our freedom to an enemy, because we believe that God has forgotten us.

***

I looked back, up at Jerusalem, her beautiful walls - my beloved home. He had thrown this all away. Even as I had walked down from Jerusalem, a part of me had known Ahaz would ruin us.

The stupid, foolish man. I snapped. I kicked the stone in front of me in anger and it landed near the generals. Now everyone was looking at me.

"Is it not enough to try the patience of humans? Will you try the patience of my God also?"

Everyone was silent: the soldiers had stopped their banter; the sky was eerily quiet.

I waited for God to speak.

God's word came to me: He would give them a sign, but not one they wanted. A single woman would become pregnant and give birth to a boy, naming him God-with-us as a sign of faith in God's protection. Before the child was able to distinguish right from wrong, while he was still toddling about, Damascus and Ephraim would be finished as nations and we would be safe. Assyria would decimate them.

At this point, I could see the king's eyes brighten. He was congratulating himself for his strategy.

"But that is not all," I said, trying to keep my anger in check as I spoke. "The trouble with befriending a bully is that they will always bully you, too. Your great saviour, the man whose parties you want to be seen at, Tiglath-Pileser III of Assyria: he will *destroy* your kingdom. He will take a razor to our precious nation and shave it so closely there will be nothing left. Nothing of the riches you have stored up in your palace now, nothing of the prosperity and safety you currently enjoy. We'll be forced to live off goats' milk-curds and honey, the only food we can find in the wilderness."

The stupid, stupid man.

I looked over at the two armies swarming on the other side of the valley, and I shook my head in frustration.

"You've made the wrong friend, and you're fearing the wrong enemy. This child, Immanuel, will be a sign to you of just how quickly these countries will be destroyed. Before the kid can spell his own name, the threat of Ephraim and Syria will be over. If only you could have waited just a little while longer..."

The king was bristling with anger at having been humiliated, and one of the bigger generals began walking towards us. I took my son's hand, trembling, and marched back with him to Jerusalem, my heart thumping all the way.

***

Why had God asked me to bring Shear-Jashub when the news had not been good, after all? Shear-Jashub - a remnant will return, I said to myself as I climbed back to Jerusalem.

Then it clicked: my son's name was a sign that as a nation we will be destroyed, but not completely. Perhaps it was not for his benefit but mine that Shear-Jashub was there today - to remind me that there is always hope, however slim. He asked me why I gripped his hand so tightly and I could only shake my head in reply.

To reflect on:

"Therefore the Lord himself will give you a sign: the virgin will conceive and give birth to a son, and will call him Immanuel. He will be eating curds and honey when he knows enough to reject the wrong and choose the right, for before the boy knows enough to reject the wrong and choose the right, the land of the two kings you dread will be laid to waste."

Isaiah 7:14-16

For further reading:

Isaiah 7:1-25

Note:

Syria and Israel were indeed conquered by Assyria soon after Isaiah's prophecy, though Judah managed to mostly hold off a disastrous Assyrian invasion. This came at a cost. 2 Kings 16:7-13 describes how Ahaz used the temple treasury to pay off Assyria. Even this protection-money wasn't enough, and it seems Assyria required Judah to introduce the worship of Assyrian gods in the Lord's temple. 2 Chronicles 28:20-21 wryly states that Assyria gave Ahaz 'trouble, instead of help'. Later, when Hezekiah was king, Assyria besieged several towns in Judah. Assyria would have conquered Jerusalem had it not been for Hezekiah's prayer, Isaiah's prophecy and God's miraculous intervention.

See the notes on Isaiah for interpretative issues on Immanuel.

Gideon is known for putting out a fleece to test God's promise to him. It was a literal fleece of sheepskin: at first, he asked God to cover the fleece with dew, leaving the rest of the ground dry; the second time he asked God to cover the ground with dew, leaving the only the fleece dry. God indulged him, and Gideon finally trusted God (Judges 6:36-40).

Over to you:

1. "This is what we do when we fear. This is what we do when we feel we have been waiting for God for too long. We make treaties. We sign away our freedom to an enemy, because we believe that God has forgotten us." It takes extreme courage to wait for God to act - especially when the enemy is at your gate. It feels like foolishness. When have you felt foolish for waiting for God to act?

2. Have you ever done the equivalent of 'making treaties' with the wrong person or thing because you had given up waiting for God?

3. Baz and the Short Wait for War
Isaiah's Story (Isaiah 8:1-18)

No one likes a prophet to tell them of disaster. That could be why my heart was beating faster than usual. But, I reasoned, truth is like eating green vegetables: we need it, even if we don't like it.

My mouth felt dry and my hands sweaty as I walked through Jerusalem on a particularly busy market day, though I smiled politely as we caught sight of people we recognised. Nevi'a shifted the baby onto her other hip, and I held Shear-Jashub's hand as we drew closer to the centre and the crowds bustled round us.

I thought back over the year. My life had changed dramatically since that day I had confronted Ahaz. The Lord had told me the time for grieving my first wife was over and I was to remarry. Literally a match made in heaven, every day I thanked God for Nevi'a, not only because I had missed being married, but because she herself was a prophet who sought the Spirit of God and loved truth above all else.

She had sleek black hair and dark eyes and, though she was slight in body, she was not to be underestimated. Every day, I saw something in her spirit that matched mine, and her strength rallied my inner reserve. Being the lone voice for so long had been hard. Now we challenged the institution together. She was walking beside me, keeping up with my pace, and I kept sneaking glances at her.

"Hey!" Nevi'a yelled.

Immersed in a reverie of my wife's virtues, I had inadvertently bumped into the object of my affection.

I apologised, and we continued on our way. A breeze blew, wafting rotting fish and vegetable leaves. As if in protest, the baby whimpered, while Nevi'a whispered soothing noises.

I had prophesied over him. Uncannily, God gave me almost the same words for him as for Ahaz's sign, the Immanuel-child.

I wondered: following this God-ordained marriage and prophecy, could it be that our baby was God's sign to Ahaz? I was convinced - right up to the point when God instructed me to name him something quite different.

I paused as we approached the palace square: in the centre were jostling traders; huddles of men throwing dice and laughing together; women haggling over the price of pomegranates; plump children playing. But if you let your eye drift out from the centre of the hubbub there was quite a different story: scarred faces; pale eyes; ragged clothes. Flies swarmed around festering wounds, hands were cupped into begging bowls. That morning, the shouts of the sellers and consumers drowned the cries of the beggars.

With a bird's eye view of the square, you could see a crowded centre, crowded edges and a tiny gap between the two spheres. An invisible bubble separated the poor from the popular. Over the past few years, the metaphorical and literal gap between the two groups had been widening.

Out from the temple emerged a clutch of Jerusalem's elite women - government officials' or rich landowners' wives, maybe, judging from their clothes. They wear all the best designer robes - beautiful silk scarves, jangling gold anklets, and their ears drip pearl earrings. They talk at top volume, as though they know everyone's watching them, (because everyone is watching them), apparently deaf to the pleas for spare change. The poor are at their feet, but all the blind man hears from them is the smug clink of gold charms on their wrists.

It's the juxtaposition that kills me.

You've got to understand: this is a nation that boasts of its welfare system as being the best around and prides itself on being a true God-fearing nation. But look at the edges and you find disabled people, refugees, single mothers and elderly widows, abandoned without financial support.

Our political leaders boast of our rich faith heritage and God's many blessings to us as a nation while ignoring the most vulnerable in society. The poor get poorer while the rich get richer.

***

We entered the square and settled ourselves near both the palace and the temple, the political and spiritual centres of our nation. My wife nodded at me. This looked like the best place; there was a good crowd. I turned my back to the buildings, faced the crowd, and together Nevi'a and I unrolled the huge scroll, holding it between us so everyone could see.

People started gathering, perhaps hoping for a street performance.

"Maher-Shalal-Hash-Baz," they read. It had been written, in faith, before our son was even conceived, and it was witnessed by Uriah and Zechariah, priest and prophet. It was a risky step - we'd married that day.

It was extreme optimism to assume we'd have a baby at the end of nine months. But sure enough, he was born right on cue, and after his miraculous arrival, we felt obliged to call him the name God had given: Maher-Shalal-Hash-Baz. (We call him Baz, for short.)

Someone nearby read it out. "'Quick to the plunder, swift to the spoil.' Who's getting plundered?"

That was the question we'd been waiting for. As the crowd surrounded our impromptu placard, I looked down the valley towards the pool of Shiloah, in our beautiful land, and I raised my voice to speak.

"This people has rejected the gentle waters of Shiloah," I said.

Judah had rejected God's gentle help. Instead of asking God to defeat Rezin, king of Aram, and Remaliah, king of Ephraim, we had put our trust in Tiglath Pileser III.

"So instead God will bring a flood - a flood from the river Euphrates, from the land of Assyria."

We could have had life-giving water from God; instead, we would have a destructive flood from Assyria. (I just hoped they realised I was speaking in metaphor. It would be unfortunate to have a panic-buy of sandbags).

Already I heard a titter in the crowd.

"Assyria is our best ally, you fool. It's the smartest thing we did to sign that treaty."

This is how I am to most people: a fool. I see peace when others see war, and war when others see peace, and for this I am labelled naïve.

I took a breath then held up my baby. There was a collective 'ahh' from the crowd.

"His name is Maher-Shalal-Hash-Baz: Quick-plunder, Swift-spoils," I yelled. "Who's getting plundered? It's us - Judah. War is coming to us. It's going to happen soon."

"All this scaremongering," I heard a woman say. She tossed her head in annoyance. Her hair, perfectly conditioned with immaculate curls, bounced around her shoulders. It was one of the silk scarf crew tutting her disapproval. "It doesn't help the unity of the nation. Unpatriotic: that's what this little speech is. You should have more faith in God. God is with us - Immanuel."

There was a murmur of approval from the crowd.

"God is with us - yes, but not in the way you think," I said to the heckling woman. "Ultimately the enemies of God - Aram, Ephraim, even Assyria - will be shattered. The flood will come up to our neck, but we shall not all perish. God is not powerless and he will rescue a few."

I looked directly at the woman, "But you need to know: there is war coming to your comfortable, rich lives, and it is coming sooner than you can possibly imagine."

The silk-scarf-woman locked eyes with me, furious. Then she glanced at a huddle of homeless people, as if fearing they would start a riot, then whispered to two of her friends, and they all flounced away from the square. I wondered if, tomorrow, I would have an official on my door reprimanding me for disturbing the peace. I didn't care. Someone had to say this.

I handed Baz back to Nevi'a, and she put her spare arm through mine and stood beside me.

The law-enforcers were getting twitchy at the corner of the square; the crowd was growing too great for their liking. Possibly Silk-Scarf-Woman had called on them to disperse us. I pulled Shear-Jashub and Nevi'a close to my side and stood my ground.

Some of the crowd watched us thoughtfully. They wanted a sign that what I was saying was true. What could I give them? They wanted a miracle, a Moses - but I was no Moses. I prayed fervently for a miracle, and there was only silence. I could feel the crowd's eyes on me. I turned to my wife and sons, who were also looking up at me. What a family we were: Nevi'a - the prophetess; baby Baz - swift to the plunder; Shear-Jashub - a remnant would return; Isaiah - the Lord is salvation. There would be no miracle, no sign, other than us.

I raised my voice as loudly as I could:
"Here am I, and the children the Lord has given me. We are signs and symbols in Israel from the Lord Almighty, who dwells on Mount Zion."[4]

Looking at the faces in the crowd, I couldn't help but feel that free bread raining from heaven would have been a more convincing sign.

***

Back at home, I hold both my children close to me, and from the window I watch the storm clouds hovering.

This call to be a prophet, it's not a part-time thing. It is not enough to carry a message: I live it out. It affects my whole family. Before my baby even learns right from wrong, Aram and Israel will be old news. One day Assyria, which King Ahaz is currently fawning over like it's the saviour of the world, will be plundering our nation. There will be death, distress and desolation. This is the truth I carry and it weighs heavily upon me.

[4] Isaiah 8:28, NIV

Every day, Baz grows a little bigger, and every day the dread in my heart grows. This country is sleepwalking into horror, and still they will not listen. But I know, and I wait - and I try to hold back the fear.

Little Baz, a child who is still babbling in innocence, is simultaneously shouting to a slumbering world that we need to turn back to God. His very presence is a potent warning.

Sometimes I think about the child called Immanuel, God-with-us. I wonder why God told me to tell Ahaz that the sign-child's name would be Immanuel, but then ours ended up being called Baz. There could be two children, perhaps. If it were not Baz, then who? Could it be Ahaz's son? Or an unknown child, growing among us in Jerusalem? Maybe Immanuel is Baz's secret middle name - the promise that God will not abandon us, even while he judges this nation for our sins.

I would be grateful for another sign-child: one who proclaimed peace, not disaster. Perhaps he will come. But probably not in my lifetime.

I stroke my son's hair, look outside at the darkening clouds, and I wait.

To reflect on:

"Here am I, and the children the Lord has given me. We are signs and symbols in Israel from the Lord Almighty, who dwells on Mount Zion."

Isaiah 8:18

For further reading:

Isaiah 8:1-18

Over to you:

1. "This call to be a prophet, it's not a part-time thing. It is not enough to carry a message: I live it out." How are you challenged by this today?

2. "I would be grateful for another sign-child: one who proclaimed peace, not disaster." Today our world is not so different to Isaiah's - countries are making treaties, or making wars, and we know not what will happen in the future. Globally, we are often waiting in uncertainty, and it is hard to know who to fear or trust. We do know Jesus, however, the ultimate sign-child, who was the definition of God-with-us and the prophesied Prince of Peace. This reminds us God is for peace, not war; unity, not division. As you take time to

pray for the world, give thanks for the character of God, who loves peace, and pray for peace in your city, country and the world.

4. The Long Wait for Light
Isaiah's Story (Isaiah 9:1-7)

I awoke in the middle of the night, pooled in sweat and fighting off invisible attackers. It took a while to become fully conscious, and I kept seeing the last image in my mind again and again: a monster wearing a crown, grinning, with blood dripping from its teeth.

In the darkness, I listened to the steady breathing of Nevi'a and the children; I told myself it was all okay. But really, it was not okay. Though I didn't know exactly when, I was sure that war was coming to our land. My nightmare-attackers could soon be real soldiers. Every day, as the king ignored me and pursued his foolish foreign policy, I grew increasingly frustrated. I spoke louder, but still the people would not listen. Torn between my anger at my people for ignoring me and pity for them because of the bad leadership they were under, my emotions were threatening to paralyse me.

"We need a better king," I muttered into the silence. It was pointless saying it out loud, but it felt good to do so anyway. My eyes adjusted to the gloom of the night and I could see a single thin beam of light lighting up the wall near the door. Carefully, quietly, I crept from my bed. I followed the light outside, closing the door behind me.

***

It was a cold, crisp night, and with few noises from animals and insects it was an unusually quiet night, too. I leaned against the doorpost and breathed awhile, trying to calm myself down, and the voice of the Lord came to me. That's often how the Lord comes: when you have waited for ages and no longer expect him, that's when it happens. There, in the middle of the quiet darkness, I heard the Voice promise, 'Light will come'.

By the light of the moon, I could just about see the roofs of Jerusalem. From this angle, they all looked packed together and seemed pressed tightly into the mountain beyond. The distances between them were significant, but they looked so close from here. The eye condenses them together into a two-dimensional picture of rectangles and triangles, and the spaces between them disappear.

Sometimes I wondered about the prophecies I received from God. They all seemed so immediate, but perhaps time in God's eyes is condensed as closely as those houses seem. If I could step into God's timeline perhaps I would see the prophecy stretching over many, many years.

Maybe in prophecy I was looking to a further horizon without realising it. I rested my hand on the wood of the doorpost. I stroked the wood while I mused, my fingers tracing its rough ridges.

It was a hard thought that perhaps I would not live to see the fulfilment of these prophecies I'd staked my reputation on.

On the other hand, my prophecies were so gloomy that it would be a bittersweet victory to be saying 'I told you so.' I would prefer that the people repented and peace remained.

I looked up at the moon, which was strangely big and bright tonight. I had always loved the moon; its light is more subtle and pure than the brash sun. Here, in the middle of the night, it felt as though I were the only one to witness it. It was just me, God and the moon.

***

I stopped myself, suddenly, mid-thought. This is what all poets do, I thought. They gaze at the moon while others make plans. I remembered the sneer of the army officials every time I delivered a prophecy. They see themselves as the ones who actually do the work of keeping a nation safe, so I am no more than a foolish idealist who has no idea about politics. Was I indeed naïve, as they believed?

But then I remembered the defeat of Midian, part of our nation's history. We shouldn't have won. All the best war analysts in the world would agree we should have surrendered. Gideon was hardly an inspirational, strong leader to lead people into battle, and he only had 300 warriors to fight Midian's 135,000. That's 300 soldiers against 135,000. It was madness to have gone to war; we should have made a deal beforehand. But - God.

It's so easy to go about our lives, making plans, relying on strategies, forgetting God has the power to reverse all expectations and work miracles. God does the unexpected and today, in our time, God would surprise us again.

It didn't matter how much the authorities planned and predicted. I had been entrusted with the words of God, and we needed that more than anything else.

Once again, I remembered that day in the temple and my commitment to keep preaching, even when the people rejected my message. I needed to shift my eyes upwards towards my creator, not downwards to my critics. I looked up to the moon again, guilt-free.

***

At that moment, a series of images flashed before my eyes. In the first, there were peoples of all colours, ages and countries rejoicing together, raising a chorus of freedom. Something good had happened - they were dancing and happy.

"Why? What's happening, Lord?"

The next image came: thousands of soldiers' boots and uniforms, browned with dried blood, were being flung onto a big fire. There were no bodies, no dead. Instead, it was the death of the fighting clothes; the end of war. They were using the fire to wilt the metal swords and shape them into farming tools.

This was why they were so happy, all those people. It was clear that this new community did not need to fight any longer: no weapons, no shields, no enemies. It would be the end of warfare. Peace would reign. What a vision! Clearly, God knew my heart's desire.

I took a few steps away from my door and climbed a small wall, standing there for a while to look over the sleeping city of Jerusalem. My heart had leapt at the thought of an end to strife. What if Jerusalem could really live up to its name and become the place of peace, where all nations would be welcomed to live under God's love?

However, when I considered the rulers in place, I had no idea how this would be possible. We would need a grand revolution.

"How, Lord?" I whispered. "How will this peace come?"

Another image flashed before my eyes: this time a smiling baby, wearing a crown. The crown was so big for his head that it dangled halfway across his face. It was a coronation ceremony - but for a baby, which seemed utterly ludicrous. I could hear the Voice naming him with his royal titles: Wonderful Counsellor, Mighty God, Everlasting Father, Prince of Peace.

The wind fluttered the leaves in the trees, like distant applause. I paused to consider the possibility: a royal baby. This would be the King to end all kings. But a baby who was called 'Mighty God'? God - the Almighty Creator - as a baby? The absurdity of the vision unsettled me.

Yet this was the kind of king that we needed. Not Ahaz, with his short-sighted plans and disregard for the safety of his people. Not the King of Assyria, full of trickery and destruction. This would be a Prince of Peace. This would be God.

Could God be referring to Hezekiah? Or the child Immanuel, perhaps growing up among us? Would this new king come so quickly? I looked back at the houses and the mountain, reflecting again on the distance between the landmarks.

I sighed. Perhaps it would be another child born, further in the future, who would ultimately be the greatest King, God with us. I stood for a while at the entrance to my house, listening to my breathing, in and out, as I also listened for the voice of God.

It was a beautiful night, and this was a beautiful promise. But there was one question left in my mind.

"How long?" I whispered. I needed to know whether I would see this peace. My heart longed for it.

"How long, O Lord?" I spoke the words out loud in a reedy and broken tone.

I waited awhile, looking out into the night sky, listening for the voice of God. I heard nothing aside from the leaves in the trees and the faint, consistent tambourine of the cicadas. The stars winked at me in the blackness, and the moon continued to shine. I stood there for a few minutes more, listening for a voice that never came, then turned from the night and went back to bed.

To reflect on:

"For to us a child is born,
To us a son is given,
And the government will be on his shoulders.
And he will be called
Wonderful Counsellor, Mighty God, Everlasting Father, Prince of Peace."

Isaiah 9:6

For further reading:

Isaiah 9: 1-7

Over to you:

1. 'Wonderful Counsellor, Mighty God, Everlasting Father, Prince of Peace' - which of those aspects of Jesus' character do you most need to remember today?

2. "The voice of the Lord came to me. That's often how the Lord comes, when you have waited for ages and no longer expect him - that's when it happens." Has that been true of your experience?

3. Isaiah saw the promise of the future King, God with us, but had no idea of how long it would take for Jesus, the true 'Immanuel', to appear. Likewise, we have been given the promise that Jesus will come again, but we have no idea how long that will be. How might we remember that Christ's return is a constant possibility?

5. The Long Wait for Peace
Isaiah's Story (Isaiah 10:33-11:9)

Fast-forward twenty or so years. I have been serving as a prophet for about thirty years now, ever since that day in the temple. Add white hairs to my head and a slight stoop to my step, though I hold my head high.

I am still a prophet. I am still unpopular. But at least now, King Hezekiah is slightly better at listening than his predecessor.

The whole family are travelling to see Nevi'a's dying brother, and the forest offers some shade from the midday heat. We come to a clearing where a group of travellers have cut down trees to make their camp. Their dwellings have long since disappeared, and all that is left is a cluster of tree stumps, of varying heights. They make good seats so I stop awhile to rest my bones.

I consider with pride my grown-up sons: Shear-Jashub has become so tall; Baz still has his mother's eyes. Now they have their own families, and all the cousins are laughing and playing together. It is a tiring walk and a sad reason to be travelling, but it is good to be together.

***

As I take a moment to wipe my brow, the word of the Lord comes to me. My heart bursting with divine words yet lacking an audience, I beckon one of my granddaughters over and sit her on my knee.

"See these huge trees?" I say. She nods, then she lifts her chin right up, arching back her neck in order to see the top of the tree.

"They're nothing compared to the trees of Lebanon," I tell her. "Tallest trees in the world, they are - lovely wood, too."

Once, as a present from the king, I had been given a table made of cedar wood from Lebanon. It was a thing of beauty; deep red and so smooth when you ran your hands over it.

"Let me tell you a story about these trees," I say. "These trees were the tallest in the wood, and all the other trees were afraid of them. Pretty soon, these trees said to themselves, 'We're so tall nothing can ever defeat us.' But they were wrong."

Little Rebecca nods her head. They were mean and nasty trees, and she knows what would become of such trees. Already she has inherited the family's keen sense of justice. I swat a fly away from her face.

"The Creator cut them down till they were nothing but stumps, just like you see here," I say. She jumps off my lap, running her hands over the grain of the stumps.

"Was this a mean tree?" she asks me.

"No, silly," her elder brother, Aaron, joins in. "Grandpa is not really talking about trees. He's talking about nations."

I give a half-smile to them both and tug at my ever-whitening beard as I try to recall how many years have passed since I first warned the king about an alliance with Assyria. Old Ahaz always ignored me, but ever since his son Hezekiah came to the throne, things have been looking up. I almost dare to hope again.

***

"Assyria will be defeated, just like this tree," I announce. "Assyria's king believes he's invincible, but God knows better."

It feels good to say those words aloud - Assyria really would be defeated. Even the biggest, most threatening superpowers are only here for a time and then gone, while God remains throughout the years.

"But our God is invincible, and so our nation will be the victor!" Aaron shouts. He whoops around, making sword-whooshing noises. My emotional instinct is to affirm his conclusion and join his whooping for Judah and the Lord, but I pause, listen again for a while and then sigh.

"Not quite," I say. "Look here. I will show you our nation. This is what Judah will be."

I beckon the children over to another stump, side by side with the Assyria tree. Both trees have been cut down. Both are destroyed.

I love God's people, but they infuriate me. I shake my head at myself: it is 'we', not 'they'. I number among the band of God's frustrating followers. Their actions so easily could have been mine.

It is so tempting, when faced with the threat of a difficult economy, to close ranks and protect yourself rather than looking out for the poor. I understand, too, the temptation to make alliances with people rather than look to God for protection. I feel the weight of our collective sin as I consider the Judah-stump.

The children turn back to me indignantly, frightened. Everyone likes to hear that their enemies have been defeated and judged; it's not so much fun when the judgement comes closer to home.

I begin explaining to the children: God's judgement is indeed coming to Assyria, but first the axe of his judgement would fall on God's own people, because we abandoned justice and leant on foreign countries for protection instead of trusting in God.

Every time I say Baz's name - daily - I am reminded of the coming judgement: swift to the plunder, quick to the spoil. The forthcoming disaster, whenever it will happen, is never far from my mind. Our former brother-nation in the Northern Kingdom, Israel, has already been plundered, defeated, enslaved by Assyria. Its capital, Samaria, is now a mess, and though we have had our own wars with them, it has been a hard defeat to witness.

We in Judah were not much better than Israel and we will face our own plundering. We who have robbed the poor will also be robbed. But - and this is the key difference - we will not be wiped out.

***

The children still look scared as I tell them this. I listen again, wanting to offer them some kind of hope.

"Look again," I say, pointing with my finger. There is a single, small green shoot on the Judah stump: a measly, leafy hope for the future.

"This tiny shoot will grow into a great tree, with more fruit than you can imagine," I say.

"A tree?" asks Rebecca.

"A king," says her brother with more confidence, though his eyes look to me for confirmation.

I nod. "This shoot is not just any king - the Spirit of the Lord will be upon him, the Spirit of a Mighty Counsellor. He won't be like the kings of this world, out for their own power, desiring riches and war."

We don't need another king like that. I am getting old now, and I have had my fill of them. I watch Rebecca clamber across a little pile of rocks at the edge of the copse. She is so carefree, so full of life.

"We need someone who loves the poor, protects the vulnerable, defeats the wicked," I mutter to myself. "We need... Rebecca, stop! Stop! Quick, grab her!"

For my granddaughter is reaching her hand into the dark recesses of the rock pile. Shear-Jashub is already running to her, sweeping her up in his arms, checking her hands for injury. There are no signs of a snake bite. We are just on the point of sighing with relief when I spot it: first the gold-brown eyes, glinting in the sunlight, then the merest shadow of the brown stripes making a 'V' on its stumpy head. It seems to pause, its tongue flicking in and out of its mouth as the seconds pass.

Shear-Jashub and the other adults hold back the children, forming a shield with their outstretched arms. Keeping our eyes on the snake, we back away. For a while there is silence. The snake eyes us, its tongue still flickering, and we do not so much as blink.

Eventually, the snake grows bored and slides away. Still, we do not move for a couple of minutes afterwards, on edge, wondering if the snake will return. When it is declared safe, some of the children return to play, but Rebecca looks shaken.

One day, I think to myself, this will be no more. There will be no more snakes, no more Assyrias, no more attackers. I feel a burning longing for safety - for myself, for these children. One day, he will be here, this prince-child of David's family, and he will be wearing peace and righteousness, not blood and greed.

Having backed away a considerable distance from the snake, we step up the pace again, and the twigs crunch under our feet. Shear-Jashub swings his little girl up and holds her tightly, carrying her as he walks. The birds are singing in the trees, and everything feels safe again. I can see her head bobbing up and down in front of me, but then she twists round to see me.

"When will the good king come?" Rebecca wants to know. "The one who will keep us safe - how long will it be?"

How long, O Lord...?

I think back to that day in the temple, some thirty years ago now, when I first encountered God. Now my granddaughter asks the same question.

"How long...?" has been the question of my entire ministry. I kept saying things that went against the political grain, and the people kept attacking me for it. The Lord has been right: they have not listened to me. I have been disbelieved and discredited in almost every quarter.

It feels like I have been waiting to be proven right my entire life. I long to be right. But more than that, I long to be safe. I yearn for peace.

How long would this little girl - and all God's people - be waiting for this leader to come? I don't know what to tell her.

I listen for the Lord's words, but again, I hear nothing but birdsong. It seems to be the one question God does not answer.

I look at her expectant eyes.

"Just a little while longer, my love," I tell her. "Keep waiting. He will come. He will come."

The birds continue their song, uninterrupted, and we keep on walking.

To reflect on:

"But with righteousness he will judge the needy
With justice he will give decisions for the poor of the earth.
He will strike the earth with the rod of his mouth
With the breath of his lips he will slay the wicked.
Righteousness will be his belt
And faithfulness the sash around his waist."

Isaiah 11:4-5

For further reading:

Isaiah 10:33-11:9

Note:

Isaiah uses the cutting down of the tall trees of Lebanon as a picture to illustrate how God will punish Assyria (10:12). The shoot of Jesse is an illustration of the hope springing from a similarly-judged Judah (10:20-21). The people of God were held accountable for their injustice (ultimately by exile into Babylon), just as Assyria had been held accountable and declined as a superpower. Isaiah looks ahead to a messianic figure who will bring peace. For Christians, Jesus is the one who fits that prophecy.

Over to you:

1. Isaiah 11:6-9 describes peace, but the verses preceding it talk about righteousness and justice. How do these things go together? How is justice a necessary precursor to peace?

2. How does this help and inform our prayers for peace in this world?

6. General Reflections
Isaiah's Story

As you look back through Isaiah's story:

1. Which parts came to life for you in a new way?

2. Which parts most resonated with your experience?

3. Which parts challenged, troubled or encouraged you?

4. Which aspects of God's character did you glimpse in Isaiah's story?

5. Which verses would you want to memorise or meditate on further?

Some of these reflections and exercises below are repeated in the Group Bible Study.

In Isaiah's story, we remember that although God cares about us as individuals, most of the Bible focuses on communities, nations, peoples: the plural, rather than the singular. God's prophecies to Isaiah revealed a short wait for war, but a longer wait for peace.

His words help us to reflect back on the prophecies fulfilled in Jesus' birth and to look forward to the eternal peace for which we still yearn. It is a God-given longing.

6. When are you most conscious of your longing for the peace of Christ - for yourself and the world?

7. Like King Ahaz, we often want to skip the uncertainty and make treaties for earthly security. Isaiah challenges us to trust in God, even when it looks like the foolish thing to do.

    "When we cannot trust God, it suddenly makes good sense to trust our worst enemy."

    John N. Oswalt[5]

    In which areas of your life have you stopped trusting God, instead trusting your worst enemy?

    In Isaiah 1-11, we see God's:
    ~   awesome power as the Ruler on the throne,
    ~   concern for the vulnerable in society,
    ~   anger at empty religion used as a cover to disregard God's laws,
    ~   and relentless commitment and grace to an unreliable people.

Pray

Bring to God in prayer your uncertainty about your own life and the world at large.

Practise a prayer of lament. So often we tie up our prayers with a conclusion, but with some psalms of lament they often are uncomfortable to pray because they don't immediately offer hope. They merely offer up our frustration and fears to God. The challenge is to pray the uncomfortable prayer and sit with it awhile. Listen in silence to what God might be saying, and pray a reply to that.

Or if God isn't saying anything obvious, pay attention to that silence. Sit with God in the silence awhile, and grieve.

Heart-cry Prayer

Lord God, seated on the throne, we lift our eyes to you for help.
We bring to you today *[name the situation of uncertainty in your life or the world]*.
Almighty God, my soul cries out:
Please, would you do something? Won't you rise and act?
How long will this go on for? It's got to stop.
How long, O Lord? How long...?

---

[5] From John N Oswalt, *The Book of Isaiah Chapters 1-39*, The New International Commentary on the Old Testament, Eerdmans, 1986, p. 203

Benediction

May you who weep and wince at the pain of the world
Find shelter under the hem of the robe of the Almighty.

May all who lament the callous cruelties of society
Look up to God's throne of justice
And find the God who is already listening, already seeing;
Already weeping, already acting.

May the prophets of God who see the wrongs of the world
Be strengthened to keep speaking, even when it seems fruitless;
And may we, too, pay attention to God's Word,
Calling to our hearts and world today.
Amen

Praying Psalm 13

Use this psalm as a basis for your prayer, personalising the words underlined as appropriate.

For the director of music. A psalm of David.

How long, Lord? Will you forget me for ever?
How long will you hide your face from me?
How long must I wrestle with my thoughts
and day after day have sorrow in my heart?
How long will my enemy triumph over me?
[name the situations you worry about]

Look on me and answer, Lord my God.
Give light to my eyes, or I will sleep in death,
and my enemy will say, 'I have overcome him,'
and my foes will rejoice when I fall.
[name the possible consequences if God doesn't intervene]

But I trust in your unfailing love;
my heart rejoices in your salvation.
I will sing the Lord's praise,
for he has been good to me.

Music

'Dies Irae' from Mozart's *Requiem* has a wonderful juxtaposition between the furious music of the 'Dies irae, dies illa' (day of anger, day of judgement) parts and the mournful cry of 'Salva me' (a plea for salvation).

Listen to the lesser-known air from Handel's *Messiah*, 'The people who walked in darkness', followed by the more famous, 'For unto us a child is born'. As you listen, meditate on or worship Jesus.

Creative Exercise: Review

~   How are you doing with the discipline of conscious waiting, spending a little time each day waiting?

~   What does it feel like to lean into the discomfort of waiting?

SECTION THREE
John the Baptist's Story

Dealing with Doubt
Waiting for Your Life's Purpose

Prelude to John the Baptist's Story

From Isaiah's wishful eyes, we roll the clock forward approximately one century. Even as Jerusalem's king blithely proclaims "Don't worry! God lives in Jerusalem, we're safe! We've got the temple of the Lord, we'll never be defeated! We've signed a treaty with Egypt, it will be fine!", King Nebuchadnezzar is there with armies and chains.

The people of Judah are put to the sword, but the brightest and best are forcibly carried off to Babylon, including a certain Daniel, of lions-den-fame. It is the unthinkable: God's people have to wait for salvation away from their home, in an enemy land, for decades.

When they return, they are diminished. The temple is in ruins, and the replacement building never quite as good as Solomon's.

They rebuild and wait for the glory days. They never really come.

The centuries pass while they wait for God to speak - hundreds of years of silence from God.

Then, perhaps seven hundred years after Isaiah consoled his grandchildren, we see a hairy and restless man in the middle of nowhere.

His name is John, and he is the greatest prophet of them all. (At least, that would have been the case if only he hadn't been overshadowed by one of his relatives.)

1. The Disappointment
John's Story (Luke 1:57-80)

For as long as I can remember, I have felt like an outsider. I don't say this for you to pity me, I say it to explain who I am.

One of my earliest memories is when I was four or five, standing alone by a tree, picking at the bark, feeling its texture, whilst the other children played noisy games in the field. I watched them awhile, then returned to the tree and noticed a spider spinning a web between two branches. Rather than the sweaty exhilaration of children, it was the spider's patient geometry that captivated me.

No two webs are alike, and yet the spider feels her path naturally. Starting with the spokes of the wheel, she links them together with loping arches; softer than silk, stronger than rope. She has no fear, she simply does what she was created to do. I could have watched her for hours. Possibly I did.

I was interrupted by my mother's hand on my shoulder.

"Little wolf," she murmured fondly. "We should have named you Wolfling." Her hands stroked my head briefly, but I flinched at her touch. She smiled at me, but her eyes held concern.

Certainly I am hairy and lean enough to be a wolf, but it wasn't this she was commenting on. I have always been someone who pulls away from others.

***

It's like this: if you are known as a child of promise, everyone wants to know you and, more than that, they want to touch you.

My childhood was full of strangers' eyes on me in the temple; older men slapping me on the back, a look of wonder in their eyes; women claiming to be distant aunts, their thick arms pulling me to their breast, plump hands squeezing my cheeks, tickling my chin and attempting to ruffle my tangled hair.

Their glances to one another, their weighty expectations, their hands and desperate eyes surrounded me throughout my childhood. Enveloped by spectators rather than friends, I was a museum piece in my own life.

There was a pause after everything I uttered, just so they could test the words as prophecy and look for deeper meanings.

This gets a bit embarrassing when you are saying things like, "Would you like some bread?" I was just being polite, but sometimes people would launch into a two-hour heated theological discussion on the topic of bread in the Torah, as though they hoped to impress me. (Really, there is only so much you can say about bread.) I never knew how to respond. After a while, much to my mother's chagrin, I stopped offering food, other than pointing, and left it to my parents to be hospitable.

***

Perhaps it would have helped if I hadn't so consistently disappointed them. At family gatherings, I would see it coming. The distant relatives would whisper and nudge my father and, wearily, he would wave his permission to go ahead and ask their questions.

"Are you Elijah?"

How is a six-year-old supposed to answer that? Though I was brighter than most, I had barely finished memorising the psalms and hadn't even started the Kings yet. I knew the story well, though, mainly because relatives were always quoting Elijah's story to me. Sometimes I wished for a cave to hide in - but there was no Queen Jezebel chasing me, just these endless questions from God's people.

"Who is the Messiah?"

Again, I need to emphasise - I was six at the time. A child. How was I supposed to know who the Messiah was? I just shrugged, though I noticed that this particular question would always bring a smile to my mother's lips. She never spoke, but ever since her pregnancy I knew she had her own theories about who the Messiah would be. (She turned out to be right, of course.)

When I gave my surly answers, the guests grew unsettled, they avoided my gaze. They didn't know what to do with me, and I didn't know what to do with them.

The same questions came, year after year. As I grew older I liked the questions less. My lack of knowledge frustrated them, and it frustrated me. Each time, they looked hopeful that I would change and grow into the specific Messiah they had imagined, or at least the longed-for prophet to call down fire upon Roman heads.

It went on like that until the Incident, which my father thereafter referred to as 'The Black Day'. I was thirteen, and all the family were gathered for Passover. Great Uncle Mordecai was there - a man I only ever saw at family reunions. His beard always smelt of slow-drying meat, and he chewed his food for longer than I thought necessary, or even possible. The food must have fully liquidised in his mouth by the time he swallowed.

Anyway, that Passover he raised his voice and theatrically asked me what I thought the Holy Spirit was saying to our fine nation today. I stalled for time, chewing on the lamb, while all eyes were on me. Then something in me snapped, and I decided for once I would tell the truth.

I looked him straight in the eye. I told him our High Priest was utterly corrupt, we had forgotten our heritage as wanderers and we were, figuratively speaking, in bed with the Egyptians.

The room went silent.

My father's face was paler than I'd ever seen it. I knew I'd misstepped, but I didn't quite know how. Wondering if belated politeness would help, I even offered him more bread. (It didn't help.)

He asked; I answered. How was I to know that he happened to be best friends with the High Priest? That was just unfortunate. The rest of the meal was awkward, to say the least.

After that, I kept my mouth shut. My silence was offensive, but less offensive than saying what I really thought.

***

Years passed, my hair grew longer, unkempt and wild, and I found that although strangers' eyes still stared, their arms no longer embraced me. I did my duty, took my turn in the temple service, learnt my Scripture diligently, but village life smothered me. While the girls giggled about who they would marry, I looked for errands that would take me on long walks in the hills. When my parents didn't need me, I killed time by writing Scripture verses in the dust with a stick, experimenting in secret with how much I could memorise. I wanted to kick against the gossip at the butcher's, the insular attitudes and hypocrisy.

***

I was restless.

I unsettled others. After years of praising me as a hero, the gossip about me turned sour. The villagers had reached the end of their patience. Hidden in the upper branches of a tree where I had fled to get some peace, I overheard the women discussing me in their huddles. They were each uniquely weighed down with shopping and weariness, each with their disparate hardships and joys, but they were united in their love of dissecting my character.

"The miracle birth, the son of a priest - it is clear that God is with him and he will do great things."

"But he's so…unfriendly."

"Downright taciturn, if we're honest."

"And there's been no mention of a betrothal, has there? Doesn't that strike you as curious?"

At this point they all tutted. It wasn't for want of trying on the part of the village girls, but my father still believed I was special, and he wanted my marriage to match that. I certainly was in no hurry to get married just to fit societal norms.

"But just think of all the years we have been under the power of the Romans. Surely it is time for the release of our people? We need someone tough to be our new warrior. Perhaps a little surliness is a small price to pay."

"I'm not sure. He's a little wilder than I think a prophet should be."

"Like Elijah? Come on, he was a wild one."

"Pah. He's no Elijah. Can you really imagine him confronting Herod? He wouldn't be let in the gates."

I had placed an internal bet on when the word 'Elijah' would come up, and it was even sooner than I thought. I watched their heads bobbing together as the women debated me.

"Well, perhaps he is too wild - now. But when he goes to the temple for his service, settles into his role as a priest, learns to respect his elders, maybe he can turn into a leader worthy of our great nation."

"Do you really think he is the Promised One, the Messiah…?"

On and on they went; I heard them, but did not speak.

***

It is a hard thing to block out someone else's doubts on your calling, especially when you're too young to really know who you are. Their words would return to me at night when I tried to sleep. I vacillated between wanting to prove them right and wanting to rebel against their plans for my life.

I kept waiting - waiting for things to become clearer. I tried to listen to God, but the clamour of their voices drowned out the flute of the Spirit. Time went on, and still I waited to become something I wasn't. Everywhere I turned I was disappointing someone.

Finally, I left.

I was supposed to be going to Jerusalem with the others to start the life that everyone expected of me. Instead, I chose the dusty road to the desert and disappeared.

To reflect on:

"And you, my child, will be called a prophet of the Most High;
for you will go on before the Lord to prepare the way for him."

Luke 1:76

For further reading:

Luke 1:57-80

Over to you:

1. When have you felt like an outsider, especially in church? How does John's story speak to you?

2. If you know Elijah's story, what parallels do you see between him and John the Baptist?

2. The Destroyer
John's Story (Luke 3:1-14)

It was in the wilderness that I finally found my place. From the first day, the vastness of the desert relieved me, and I was happy to surrender myself to its sound and space.

I noticed each subtle change of light. Against the sandy rocks, the colours of the sky danced like an ever-changing canvas. Azure, grey, white: I noticed how the sky moved, subtly, though we normally barely notice it. Then, to punctuate the beginning and ending of the day, the sun spilled orange, crimson and fuchsia as the molten gold sphere pushed up the sky-waters at dawn or dipped below the earth at dusk.

Now that I had no human interaction, my ears became attuned to the pad of a jackal's paws prowling over the rocks, the flap of a vulture's wings overhead.

The shade of the broom tree became my home and my protection. Each day, I watched the sun make its course in the heavens: the long shadows grow ever shorter the midday sun becomes almost - but not quite - unbearable, and with relief the shadows lengthen again. Day after day, the pattern was the same, and I learned to love both light and shadow.

***

In the wilderness, I waited. There were spiders everywhere, when you stopped to look, and creatures scuttled across the earth. Spiders span their webs, bees buzzed about their nest, and they paid no attention to me. The jackal does not care if you look different. The raven does not want to make small talk. Every creature goes about its business, and God sees each one.

Gradually, I forgot about the pain and frustration of family arguments. The desert is a great cure for self-obsession. When you've spent enough time in the wilderness, you start to care less about what people think of you.

I woke with the sun; I slept with the stars. The days blurred into months, years and, while my muscles grew tauter, my breathing became slower and deeper. More air, more freedom - I breathed it all in.

I learnt to follow the ibex, who always seemed to know where to find water. The energy of the warm winds calmed me, and the whisper of God's own breath seemed to accompany them.

Even the fear of beasts made me feel more alive than ever. Every time I heard the howl of a hungry wolf or a snake's fierce hiss, I was more aware than ever of my need of God as my protector.

The openness of the desert landscape helped me to see with my spirit rather than my body. I learnt to live in harmony with my surroundings and keep in step with creation's rhythm. I ate what I could find - locusts and honey - until food became merely fuel for me. My hair and beard grew yet longer, a matted mess in the dusty desert wind, and my clothes began to blend in with the surroundings. I walked with God and felt gloriously alive.

In the village I was wild; in the wild I was filled with peace.

***

With the slightest shadow of a dark cloud, the lizards would skitter and the birds flee. I started to see the ways that God, as conductor, oversees and brings together the various sections of creation to play new melodies, and I worshipped God for it.

It crept up on me - the conviction that I could be one of God's instruments, my song an important one. There, in the home of the wolves and hyenas, I began to own my voice and calling. I may have been the only one in Israel whose heart burned for justice, impatient for the people to snap out of their complacency and come back to God, but I no longer cared about being an outsider.

Neither did I fear being hated for my prophecy. Throughout the years in the wilderness, in the absence and silence, the words had built up inside me, and I could contain them no longer.

In the silence of the wilderness, I found my voice. I now understood what God had wanted for me. My role was not to sing soothing birdsong. My message was a howl to disturb the night and prepare people for the dawn.

***

One day, I knew the moment was right: I opened my mouth and did not hold back. The strangest thing was that now, when I called my people a brood of vipers, they listened, they nodded, they couldn't get enough of it. After the long wait in the wilderness, God had opened the way for me to speak.

Believers always want grand, happy vocations: to be a beneficent ruler, steady hands, a sunbeam for God. They sing songs about it. No one sings "God wants me for a destroyer". Yet that is what I was, clearing mountains, filling valleys, stirring up hearts of God's people to believe.

This wasn't about defeating the government, maddening though it was to see God's nation ruled by people who derided the Lord. This was about purifying the hearts of God's family, not enemies. I was called to flatten those mountains and roadblocks of complacency and sin, so the Messiah could travel into a country of a cleansed people, hungry for God's justice.

Day after day, the hand-wringing, anxious middle-classes would come out to the desert, bringing their guilt and earnestness. They came like tourists, all eager to catch sight of this prophet who was undoubtedly hairier and more abrupt than they expected.

The crowds kept coming, every day still more, and my voice grew louder.

I was inviting them to a funeral, a ritual of repentance. Every day I stood in the waters, my legs growing numb with the cold. Some of them never left. They wanted to be near me, to be like me, to follow me. The numbers grew every day - sinners coming for purification, followers desperate for a leader.

The fans started getting excited.

"Look how many are coming, master! Everyone is listening to you!"

The crowds kept coming, but the multitudes didn't matter to me, because I had my eyes fixed on the one person who would someday walk over the horizon. The time was coming; I could feel it in my bones.

Every morning, I prayed as I walked. I was waiting for that moment, always waiting. The spiders' webs sparkled with crystal dew in the morning light.

He will come, I told the air. He will come.

***

When he came, it was a day like any other. I was down by the river, baptising repentant sinners. As I looked up, over the horizon, I spotted him immediately, surrounded by his own followers. He was here; the wait was finally over. There was nothing particularly special about his walk or appearance that singled him out as the Messiah. But the Spirit within me knew and leapt in my chest. Before I knew it, I was leaping, too.

To reflect on:

As it is written in the book of the words of Isaiah the prophet,
"A voice of one calling in the wilderness,
'Prepare the way for the Lord,
Make straight paths for him.
Every valley shall be filled in,
Every mountain and hill made low.
The crooked roads shall become straight,
The rough ways smooth.
And all people will see God's salvation.'"

Luke 3:4-6

For further reading:

Luke 3:1-14

Over to you:

1. 'The jackal does not care if you look different.' What lessons have you learned about God or yourself from the natural world?

2. 'No one sings, "God wants me for a destroyer."' Although John was the particular fulfilment of the prophecy to prepare the way for Jesus, who can you think of today like John who is a 'godly bulldozer', destroying obstacles to faith and salvation?

3. In my retelling, John was able to ignore the pressure of the multitudes because he was concentrating solely on Jesus. How does this speak to you today?

3. The Doubter
John's Story (Luke 3:15-22)

I crouched in my putrid jail cell, head between my hands, waiting for the messengers to return. Today the stench of rot overpowered my nostrils, and it was all I could do to keep breathing. Hyper-aware of every sound that could indicate their arrival, I heard every groan in the neighbouring cells, every footstep in the distance. Still they didn't come.

***

As I waited, I thought again of the best day of my life - the day I baptised Jesus of Nazareth. He went down into the water, and the world fell silent around me. When he emerged, spluttering, I felt the Holy Spirit as never before; I heard God speak as powerfully as one could imagine. In that one moment, I knew who I was and why my life mattered. The great words my father had spoken over me in the womb all those years ago became words of life and freedom, rather than a heavy yoke. My soul was electrified.

That was the defining moment of my life, and it felt like all heaven applauded.

Jesus embraced me and, after a brief chat, he went on his way.

Then…nothing.

***

I kept preaching, of course, as normal, but at the back of my mind, I was waiting. Before, I had been waiting for the Messiah. Now I had met the Messiah, I couldn't help wondering: why wasn't anything happening? All this time, preparation and preaching, all this investment of myself - I was ready for the explosive conclusion. I expected something big: a war, a battle, an apocalypse - a baptism of Spirit and fire.

But Jesus went on his way and carried on preaching to his followers, eating and drinking with traitor tax-collectors.

My father had begun my life by singing of long-awaited freedom, and in my bones, I carried the weight of expectation from the centuries of oppression our people had faced. We were ready: ready to be liberated.

Now the liberator was here. What was he doing?

***

I should have expected it, I suppose, but I'd somehow hoped that being on the fringes protected me from the scrutiny of the establishment. I took a risk with attacking Governor Herod, but I answer to a greater leader, and someone had to point out that you can't go around taking your brother's wife as property when she was already a blood-relation, no matter how much protection you had from the Romans. It seemed folly to remind a traitorous sellout of God's law that he should be obeying it, but I wanted to try. There was always hope of repentance, always a chance to change your mind after turning against God. Perhaps he would crawl his way back to God - if only he could be persuaded first to drop to his knees.

One day, when I was preaching and baptising as usual, the sun shone too brightly. Before I knew it, swords were flashing among the dull mass of the crowd, and then the soldiers were upon me.

"Where am I going?" I asked.

"To answer to Herod," they soldiers grunted.

With their arms pinning me, I craned my head back towards the desert one last time, my eyes scavenging the landscape for the colours and shapes that would sustain me in solitude. Breathing deeply, I filled my lungs one last time with the warm, dry air, scented with olive trees.

They dragged me to Herod's fortress.

Then, in prison, alone, I waited.

***

It was a hard adjustment. The prison cells were dank and dark, with barely any natural light: the perfect growing conditions for mould. The torches flickered uncertainly in the damp air, vulnerable to being extinguished altogether. Whenever they failed, we had to wait for a guard to notice. Sometimes it took hours.

Without being able to see clearly, my other senses were heightened. When I first got here, the smell was overpowering: urine and faeces, blood, rats, and rotting food all covered over with straw, intermingling with the air. I tried to breathe through my mouth, but then I just seemed to taste the smell. On that first day, it made me vomit, which inevitably did nothing to help the situation. I breathed in the acid while my stomach heaved.

***

For a while, I told myself it would be temporary. After all, no one was kept in prison for long. A few days, a week perhaps, and then you were dispatched - either to freedom or death. Herod was annoyed, but he also respected me. He kept inviting me up from the prison to take a meal with him while we talked. I talked with him but would not break bread with him, even though my stomach rumbled. I was his portable conscience, and when he had had his fill of truth, he would shut me away again.

No, I reasoned, he would soon release me. My followers were loyal, climbing the hills to encourage me and bring me messages and food. It wasn't usual to be kept in prison for so long - there wasn't a lot of space, and the turnover was rapid as people left, wailing, for their execution.

I waited for news that I would either be killed or released, wondering if the former was more likely than the latter as the days went on. No, I told myself, Herod is angry with me, but he also likes me. I will be freed. I waited for news of the Messiah defeating the Romans, freeing our country.

Every day, I paced the cell, using the walls and the long chains to stretch my muscles. I did everything I could to fight the atrophy, but as the days passed, I could feel my strength diminish. The food my followers brought me did not satisfy, and I grew weaker in body and mind.

Day after day I waited for news of liberation: of my personal liberation, or the greatest liberation to come.

It never came. The cobwebs gathered dust, and the days went on and turned into weeks, then months.

***

Of course, I found ways to speak, even from the fortress. I spoke the truth, as I always had, because it's the only thing I know to do. This is what it means to have the Lord's call on your life: it's what you continue to do, even in the most difficult circumstances, because you can't *not* do it. The impulse to speak coursed throughout my veins. I refused to back down and approve of Herod's marriage. I would not let the pressure of prison bend the iron of my soul.

But it all took its toll - the treatment by the guards, the food, the smells, the groans, the lack of space, the darkness. My words were still a roar, but my soul had begun to whimper.

And still there was no word from the Messiah. I replayed the memories in my head again and again, with the questions increasing each time. I had always been so sure of everything - but what if, for this one crucial issue, I had made a mistake?

This was the big question plaguing me: what if Jesus wasn't the one? What if all of my life, my preparation and prayer, had been a colossal mistake, and I had directed people's attention to the wrong person?

Doubt metastasised throughout my being.

I had once been so sure, but now the Spirit's voice sounded tinny and faint, and I was unexpectedly unsteady. In the desert I had been so strong, but now I was in captivity and growing more subdued by the day.

Finally, two of my most loyal followers asked me if there was anything they could do for me. They stood in my cell, the guard looking grumpy behind them. They came regularly, risking their freedom every time they came into the prison, because the guards could have decided that they were conspiring with me and flung them in here to keep me company.

Touched by their devotion, the question tumbled out of my mouth before I could reel it back in:

"Is he the promised Messiah, or should we expect someone else?"

I hesitated.

"I need you to ask him."

It was the question that had been pulsing in my brain for weeks, but I was surprised by how hurt my tone was when it came out of my mouth.

They stared at me in surprise, and I looked at the floor and said no more.

***

As their footsteps receded into the distance, I could feel my heart pounding. It was the most powerless I had ever felt. Asking that one question felt as though I had uttered blasphemy or revealed myself as naked. I took my head in my hands again and pushed my palms into my temples.

This much I could say for certain: of all the times in my life I have had to wait, this was the most agonising wait of all.

To reflect on:

"John answered them all, "I baptise you with water. But one who is more powerful than I will come, the straps of whose sandals I am not worthy to untie. He will baptise you with the Holy Spirit and fire.""

Luke 3:16

For further reading:

Luke 3:15-22

Over to you:

1. "The liberator was here. What was he doing?" At Jesus' baptism John was so sure of his identity and his calling, because he was sure of Jesus. Likewise, when he didn't understand what Jesus was doing, he lost some of his own sense of identity and calling. How have your own sense of identity and calling been influenced by knowing or doubting Jesus?

2. John was waiting for liberation - both personally, from jail, and for God's people, from the Romans and from their sin. How have you experienced God's liberation, and in what sense are you still waiting for it?

4. The Greatest
John's Story (Matthew 11:2-15)

As I waited for Jesus' response, my thoughts somersaulted over each other. Of all the potentially offensive confrontations in my life, this was the one that made me tremble. In my cell, I found myself shivering, where before I had not been cold. My hands shook. I had openly voiced my doubts to Jesus and to the crowd.

What would he say? Messiah, or not? I couldn't work out which would be worse: if he was indeed the Messiah, then I would have revealed myself as the questioner, the doubter. If he were not the Messiah... I dared not travel too far down that road. I had questioned whether Jesus was the Messiah, and in so doing, I had questioned my life's ministry.

***

Really, what I wanted was some sort of an apology. Some sort of action, perhaps. Or if only he could lay out the timetable for salvation. I needed confirmation that he was the Messiah, so I would know the Romans were on their way out. Finally, finally liberated, we would enjoy God's rule of peace and justice.

There was a thin blade of sunlight slicing through the slit in the stone wall above me. I fixed my eyes there and clenched my fists to stop the rising emotion. It was not only my nation that I wished to be freed. I wanted to be out there again. I wanted to feel the dry earth beneath my feet, not this urine-covered filth.

Was Jesus the Messiah? If I were honest, I wanted Jesus to answer something like this:

"Oh, yes, I am the Messiah - and you're right - I've been taking a bit too long getting to know the people. It's time for that action we've all been waiting for. Thanks for the prompt. I'm on it now."

But as soon as I identified what I wanted, I realised how arrogant I was and how foolish the question sounded. The Messiah - needing a reminder of what he should be doing? He probably got that all the time...

"This is the Messiah I want you to be. You need to be doing this."

Everyone comes to theology with their own agenda.

I had known this as a child, the burden of people's expectations placed heavily on my shoulders. I'd seen their accusing stares when I didn't match up to what they expected a child of promise to be, and I'd hated them for it. Yet I'd just done exactly the same to Jesus.

I hated myself for asking the question.

I had become my Great Aunt, with her furry eyebrows and frowning eyes, who had always prodded me and disapproved of me. Yet, if I had been able to turn back time, I still would have asked Jesus, because I so badly wanted to know the answer. I frustrated myself but could not escape myself.

In any case, it had been done. Anxiously, I tapped out rhythms on the stone, annoying the other prisoners. It was the only way to stay sane.

The hours passed, and still I waited.

***

Familiar footsteps echoed down the corridor, and I jumped to my feet as I recognised the voices of the messengers. Was Jesus the Messiah?

Yes.

No.

Yes.

No.

Yes.

No.

I weighed each possibility as they came nearer, ever more frantically. The guard let them through, and I looked into their faces.

"Yes or no?" I blurted, before even saying hello. I couldn't wait any longer: I had to know.

They looked at each other. There was an excruciating pause.

"He didn't say outright," they admitted.

Huh, I thought. A third option. What was I to do with that? I breathed out, disappointed.

"But - John - we saw such things! That's how he answered us - not with a yes or no, but telling us to pass that news on to you. The blind see, the lame walk, the lepers are healed, the deaf hear, the dead are raised, the poor are honoured. This is what he wants you to know."

I heard their words, but it was as if I were having a private conversation with Jesus himself.

He had not answered with a yes or no, but with Isaiah 35.

Resting my head against the wall, I closed my eyes, and, from the recesses of my memory, I fished out the phrases I was looking for:

"Then will the eyes of the blind be opened and the ears of the deaf unstopped.

"Then will the lame leap like a deer, and the mute tongue shout for joy."[6]

Of course. Of course. Blind people seeing; deaf people hearing; lame people walking. He was living out the day of redemption described exactly in Isaiah 35.

What came next in that chapter from Isaiah? I finished the chapter in my mind: "Water will gush forth in the wilderness and streams in the desert"[7] - that was it.

I remembered the long hours of hunting for water in the desert, desperate to find a stream. At times, it had been hard work as I grew increasingly thirsty. I had needed that water like I needed justice and freedom now. Jesus had said the life-giving streams would come - liberation would come.

He had answered me: not in facts, but with Scripture and the images of my life.

At that moment, it hit me: Jesus knew me. He knew what I was thinking. He knew what I needed to hear.

I did my utmost not to weep, but I could feel the tears springing to my eyes. I cried with grief because I had doubted, and I cried with relief that he really was the Messiah.

Still, I did not understand him. Why was I still waiting? Why had our nation not yet been liberated? But I believed, once more, that he was the one for whom the world was waiting. Jesus was the Messiah.

***

I hid my tears behind my hand as I wiped my face, and I glanced down at the murky corner of the cell. The faithful spider was crawling slowly across, and I concentrated on its movements, steadying my emotions as I breathed. For the first time since I had baptised Jesus, I caught a spark of joy in my soul again.

But as the relief of knowing Jesus was the Messiah subsided, I felt a new weight in my gut.

I had exposed myself as a doubter. I must have been a colossal disappointment to Jesus.

---

[6] Isaiah 35:5-6a
[7] Isaiah 35:6b

After all my determination to be different, I had been just the same as my hordes of disappointed disciples who had wanted me to be their saviour. After all my years of preparing people for the Messiah, I had undermined my whole purpose.

I had never felt such an utter failure as I did in that moment. I tried to watch the spider to distract myself, but it crawled into a crack in the rocks, out of sight.

My followers shuffled their feet, occasionally opening their mouths, but not yet speaking.

"Right, right," I muttered. Perhaps they hadn't noticed my tears. Maybe I could pull it off as something I had expected all along, concealing my doubt and emotions. "And did he say anything else?"

"Yes," they said.

They exchanged an excited glance, and I leaned in further to try and read their expressions.

"He talked about you - he said you were the promised messenger Malachi prophesied, who was preparing the way."

They paused to let this sink in, and I clutched my hair, pressing on my head to try to stop the emotion.

"John," they continued, "Jesus said that you were the Elijah who was to come. He said of all the humans on earth, there was none greater than you - and yet the kingdom of God would be even greater."

This time I could not hold back the tears. Not only had Jesus articulated what I wanted to hear, he had given me the message my heart truly needed.

He'd told me the truth about his identity, and he'd also affirmed my own identity. My calling was not a mistake. My life was not a mistake. In God's grace, even with my doubt and questioning, even when I had potentially insulted him, I was still called a great prophet by God's Anointed One, and he'd promised that there would be liberation in the future.

I thought again of words from Isaiah 35:

"Strengthen the feeble hands, steady the knees that give way;

"Say to those with fearful hearts, "Be strong, do not fear;

"Your God will come, he will come with vengeance,

"With divine retribution he will come to save you."[8]

Jesus knew. He knew me.

In the midst of my arrogant question, he'd spotted that my knees had been giving way, my hands had been trembling, so he had sent me the food

---

[8] Isaiah 35:3-4

I needed for strength, in the form of Isaiah 35. They were words that would sustain me for a long time, and I chewed them slowly.

I swallowed hard, wiped my tears, wiped my hands.

"Would you tell him thank you?" I said.

***

When they left, the prison was quiet again. In the dampest corner of the cell, illuminated by a sliver of light, I could see a spider spinning a web, playing with gossamer in the darkness.

To reflect on:

"Truly, I tell you, among those born of women there has not risen anyone greater than John the Baptist; yet whoever is least in the kingdom is greater than he."

Matthew 11:11

For further reading:

Matthew 11:2-15

Over to you:

1. "This is the Messiah I want you to be. Everyone comes to theology with their own agenda." What kind of Messiah do you wish Jesus was? What disturbs you, if anything, about his character and actions?

2. "I still did not understand him. But I believed…" When have you felt similarly?

3. "Not only had Jesus articulated what I wanted to hear, he had given me the message my heart truly needed." What do you see of the kindness of Jesus in his response to John's doubts? How have you seen Jesus' kindness in his dealings with you this year?

5. The Least
John's Story (Mark 6:17-29)

Even at this distance from Herod's banqueting hall, I can hear the thump of the drums through the walls as the music plays. Tonight, I am sleepless. A spider runs over my hand, and I shiver. Weeks have passed since Jesus' message, and I have been more at peace. Tonight, however, I feel alert again, like my spirit has awoken from a long nap.

If there is anything happening in this fortress, it is normally the guards who know it first. Unseen in the corridors, they stand statue-still, so you forget they are listening. Earlier today, one of the guards, a more sympathetic one, whispered to me that I might be in danger. Herod's new wife Herodias and her daughter had been plotting, he told me. It didn't look good for me.

***

My entire life has been focused on waiting for God's promises to be revealed: the long-awaited Messiah, saving his people from slavery. When at last I witnessed the coming of the Messiah, it was harder to recognise than I thought.

In this cell, hovering between freedom and death, I have been waiting for news of victory - for our nation and the world. I know now God's good kingdom will come. I hadn't considered that it might not come yet - that I might die while I was still waiting.

I had thought I was the new Elijah, preparing the way for the Messiah. Now the thought strikes me: what if I am also the new Moses - waiting on the edge of the Promised Land while Jesus, the new Joshua, saves the people?

Perhaps it is enough to have seen the Promised Land, even if I never enter it. Maybe it is enough to have known the Saviour, even if I haven't seen the fulfilment of his salvation.

***

Upstairs, the trumpets are reaching a crescendo, and I can hear distant applause. Then - abruptly - the applause stops. There is silence.

Something is not right.

Herod's parties are known for a number of things, but silence is not one of them. My stomach knots, and I grip tightly onto my chains.

The slightest whisper comes to my heart, so subtle that I hardly know whether to believe it: *it is time*. I listen out for any audible clues, but there is just a low hum of activity in Herod's hall now, no music.

The wait is over. *It is time.*

The loudest sound is my heartbeat, pulsing in my ears.

***

While I was in the desert, I knew one false move could lead to my death - a wild animal attacking, or simple dehydration. There was always the threat of death, but I didn't fear it greatly because I knew in my blood that God had more for me to do.

Now, it is different. The lame walk, the blind receive their sight - this indeed is the Messiah who was to come. In the days after the messengers came back from Jesus, I kept revisiting those precious words. Like turning a smooth stone over and over in my hands, I turned these words over in my brain. They were my fuel. Now, in the darkness, I try to hold on to Jesus' words again, and I murmur Isaiah 35 to myself, over and over:

"Then will the eyes of the blind be opened and the ears of the deaf unstopped.

"Then will the lame leap like a deer, and the mute tongue shout for joy."[9]

The fear of death grips my heart, and I clench the chains until my knuckles turn white.

I breathe slowly to calm myself and start reciting facts under my breath, as though I am rehearsing a speech in my defence.

I have cleared the final highway, and the King has been walking through it. I recall the days of wonder in that lonely desert, where God spoke to me so clearly. I ask his Spirit to be upon me now, in the dark and gloom.

---

[9] Isaiah 35:5-6a

"Water will gush forth in the wilderness and streams in the desert."[10]

This is the message Jesus gave me, and now I repeat the words to myself. In my life, I have only seen the dust and decay of this world, but at some point Jesus will bring life, true life. I grip tightly onto my chains; I grip tightly to these promises.

I have done what God wanted of me; in the end, I did not fail Him. Neither have I failed myself: I have been who I was created to be - a wild, hairy, truth-telling prophet of God.

"He must become greater; I must become less."

I once said this, comparing my ministry to Jesus'. Now, tonight, I let myself feel the full weight of those words. I must become less. Looking at my white knuckles gripping the chains, I force myself to release the chains. My arm seems to float in mid-air as the muscles relax. As the reality of my death sets in, I allow my whole body to slump, sinking down against the stone wall.

"Strengthen the feeble hands, steady the knees that give way;
"Say to those with fearful hearts, 'Be strong, do not fear[11]...'"

I whisper those words to the heavens, a half-prayer for courage.

It's a frightening thing to imagine your life slipping away, becoming no more, disappearing into nothingness. When I remind myself of where I am going, it is easier. When I die, I will not be nothing; I will be me, fully me. I will be with God, who makes everything whole and full.

By saying goodbye to this life of darkness, I will be stepping into stunning light. There is loss, but only temporarily: ultimately it will all be gain. By leaving this life of beauty and brokenness, I will walk into completeness and colour. I think again of the sunsets in the desert, a fierce sweep of fire upon the cloudless sky, and my breathing relaxes a little.

***

"Your God will come, he will come with vengeance;
"With divine retribution he will come to save you[12]."

---

[10] Isaiah 35:6b
[11] Isaiah 35:3
[12] Isaiah 35:4

My salvation has not come in the way I thought it would. I had imagined riding into Jerusalem after battle, the Messiah at my side - not enclosed in the darkness of a prison cell.

Nevertheless, I recognise my impending death for what it is: my salvation. The nation's and world's salvation would follow; I must be content with simply having handed on the baton.

***

I strain my ears to hear: up in Herod's great hall it is still quiet, but there is a gentle hubbub, as though the guests are waiting for a great performance.

I breathe slowly, in and out, calming my spirits. Then it strikes me: in a few moments I will see God face to face. All my life I have loved truth and justice, and that has made me unpopular, but shortly I will be meeting truth and justice personified. I cannot think of anything more exciting than this.

Suddenly, I burst into laughter. I have never been popular or well-liked by society. But in heaven, with the God of truth and justice, I will not be unpopular. I will belong. It's a good thought, and it feels like I'm sharing a joke with God.

At the end of the corridor, I hear the rattle of the keys. Someone is coming. His footsteps get louder as he approaches my cell.

I am done with waiting. I am ready.

I think not of my death, but of whom I will ultimately be meeting. I leap to my feet.

To reflect on:

"The bride belongs to the bridegroom. The friend who attends the bridegroom waits and listens for him, and is full of joy when he hears the bridegroom's voice. That joy is mine, and it is now complete. He must become greater; I must become less."

John the Baptist, speaking of Jesus - John 3:29-30

For further reading:

Mark 6: 17-29

Over to you:

1. "Maybe it is enough to have known the Saviour, even if I haven't seen the fulfilment of his salvation." Although we have seen more of Jesus' salvation than John the Baptist did, there is a sense in which we who live between Christ's first and second comings are still waiting for the fulfilment of our salvation. How do these words speak to you today?

2. "Shortly I will be meeting truth and justice personified." Whatever else we are waiting for, we all wait to meet Christ, either at his coming or our death. Though life is to be treasured here and now, what makes you excited about heaven and meeting God the Trinity face to face?

6. General Reflections
John the Baptist's Story

As you look back through John the Baptist's story:

1. Which parts came to life for you in a new way?

2. Which parts most resonated with your experience?

3. Which parts challenged, troubled or encouraged you?

4. Which aspects of God's character did you glimpse in John's story?

5. Which verses would you want to memorise or meditate on further?

These reflections and exercises below are NOT repeated in the Group Bible Study.

Music

This week, listen to O Come, O Come, Emmanuel (for a modern recording, try Enya, Sugarland or Pentatonix.) Also, from Handel's *Messiah*, 'Every valley shall be exalted', and 'Then shall the eyes of the blind be open'd'.

Dealing with doubt

Heart-cry Prayer:

Dear Lord
Are you actually there? Do you actually care? I don't know if I
believe. I want to, but it demands too much of me to hope. I have had
enough. My brain is so tired. I have seen too much mess, so much
confusion. It seems easier just to forget everything and close my eyes.
I'm talking to you but I don't know if you're there, or if you are good.
But I'm still talking, and I should definitely get holiness points for
that. Do you give holiness points? Are you there?
Lord - please be there. Please be good. (I really want you to be.)

Please don't judge me. Help me in my unbelief. Come to me, please, Lord. (If you are there.) Please. Amen.

Benediction

For all those with weak knees, feeble hands, fading faith -
May you know Christ's hands holding your own
Through the hands of another human.
May their strength give you strength;
May their faith give you faith,
So you can walk another day with Christ at your side.

Be strong; do not fear; your God will come.

When all around you is wasteland,
And your spirit is cracked and dry,
May you be flooded with God's Spirit,
Slaking your thirst for true life.

Be strong; do not fear; your God will come.

When you look out and see a lonely path ahead,
May you have eyes to see the company of saints, past and present;
And may you know the Spirit of God
Beside you, before you; in you, around you.

Be strong; do not fear; your God will come.

When you are weary of life;
May God give you grace upon grace
To rejoice, blossom, burst into bloom.
As unexpectedly as Christ arrived,
May your life and heart be transformed.

Be strong, do not fear; your God will come.
Amen.

Creative Exercise: A Cloud of Doubt

In my interpretation of John the Baptist's story, his experience of waiting in prison caused him to doubt that Jesus was the Messiah. After years of waiting for a baby, Sarah doubted that God would make good on his promise to her. Disappointment, delay, being left in limbo - these things can all contribute to and amplify pre-existent doubts. Sometimes it can help to articulate those doubts.

Take a blank sheet of paper. On one side write all the doubts you experience in your faith - both about who God is and God's involvement in your life. Represent them as one cloud or many clouds, thinking about their size. Cut them out, and, on the other side, colour them as you think through them and bring them to God. (If you're not into drawing, just list them or represent them in another way.)

On a separate piece of paper, draw a sun to represent whatever you know you believe. In my retelling, when he doubted in prison, John was able to return to the truths about Jesus he knew for sure - 'the blind see, the lame walk...' When doubts cloud our faith and we are unsure, it is good to identify the things we know we believe. It may not be much, but it's good to find a starting point.

~ What is that one truth (or more truths) that you are sure about when it comes to faith? Which Bible verses are your anchors, the ones you return to?
~ Write it/those on the sun and colour in the sun, praying them through as you do. (If you're not into drawing, just list them.)

Now take both pieces of paper and arrange them so that they reflect your current state of faith.

~ Are the doubts completely obscuring the sun? Are they nowhere in sight? Is your desire to put the words on the cloud face-up, or face-down?
~ When you have arranged it, consider how it feels to have done this exercise.
~ Use it as a basis for prayer, and recommit yourself and your desires to God.

SECTION FOUR
Mary's Story

Dealing with Disgrace
Waiting for Jesus

Prelude to Mary's Story

From John's death, go back in time thirty years or so, just before he was born. While he was still floating in his mother's womb, a teenager was about to find out she was pregnant.

As you read, see also in Mary's pregnancy and labour an extended metaphor for our wait for Christ's return.

1. When Heaven Waits
Mary's Story (Luke 1:26-38)

How do you measure the line between childhood and adulthood?

I pondered that question one afternoon, as I tried to make bread just like my Mama and Grandma. When I was very little, I used to watch in fascination as they baked together. With their mouths they squabble and argue, but their hands move at the same time, kneading the dough together in rhythm.

That's the way it is in our community: tradition passed from generation to generation, women reciting holy words from the Torah between gossip and disagreements over the best way to shape the Sabbath challah bread. Before I knew it, I was old enough to stand beside them, and my hands moved in rhythm with theirs.

But - alas! - I still burnt my bread at the edges.

My life thus far had been a fourteen-year preparation for the world of marriage and motherhood. What is childhood after all, if not a big race, with adulthood as the prize? If you had asked me last year if I were ready for adulthood, I would have boasted of my maturity. But now I was on the cusp of a big change, I felt more like a child than ever.

I guess that's what the betrothal is supposed to do: turn someone from child to adult in the space of a year. I was in that in-between space: newly-betrothed, but waiting to feel ready to be a wife.

***

It made it easier that it was Joseph. I'm a village girl, and people are friendly in Nazareth, so we already knew each other. He was quite a bit older than me, but his beard still looked timid and out of place on his chin, like he had yet to grow into it.

On the day of our betrothal, my parents and Joseph's mother all met together in our house. They were old friends, yet their laughter seemed louder than usual and their talk more eager. My hands felt sweaty, so I clasped them together, trying to look demure and grown-up at the same time. Suddenly, prompted by my mother's raised eyebrows, I remembered that I was supposed to be a good hostess and offer more wine and figs. I scrambled to gather everything together, while my hands trembled slightly. There were so many things to remember.

Papa cracked a barely-humorous joke which had them all guffawing ridiculously, and I sneaked a glance at Joseph. Mortifyingly, he was looking right at me. I felt my cheeks go hot with embarrassment - but then, his cheeks were turning red, too.

I realised in that moment: he was nervous, too. That helped. At that point, I suppose we could have looked away in embarrassment, but instead we broke into grins. At that moment, I saw in his eyes that he loved the Lord and was a good man. He would look after me, I knew. I whispered a prayer of thanks for the Lord's provision.

Papa took Joseph aside to deal with the money and contract and, just like that, I was betrothed. Legally, technically, I was Joseph's wife, though of course I would still be in my parents' house for a year, with time to adjust to the idea and get to know him a little.

By then, I would definitely have learnt to perfect the right spice mix for the Passover lamb and definitely not over-salt it, I told myself. After that transition year, the marriage would be - consummated - which I was determined not to be thinking about at that moment, because I didn't want my cheeks to go any redder than they already were. (I wondered if I could claim to be ready for marriage when I still blushed at the word 'consummation'.)

***

I had entered that limbo state of being married-but-not-quite, and I was improving daily at baking. My parents were delighted: my adult life was proceeding entirely as expected. It was oddly reassuring.

And then the Messenger showed up and turned everything upside down.

***

A few days later, I was alone in the house, working up a sweat sweeping the dust, humming to myself, when he came.

I had always believed in angels, but that doesn't do anything to prepare you for actually meeting one. There's no way of describing it. It's not so much the flash of light, or the life-changing message, but the feeling you get when you look at an angel. It's like a searchlight on your heart, like you're being seen naked. My legs shook of their own accord.

"Greetings, highly favoured one!" the angel said.

That made me want to turn round to check that there wasn't anyone else standing behind me. He's got the wrong girl, I thought, and then half-giggled to think that perhaps God's angel had flown to the wrong address. Maybe I could give him directions? That would be fun.

The angel continued to look at me.

"God is with you," he said.

I gave a weak smile, baffled. It was so unlikely. Didn't angels normally come to men and tell them to fight for Israel? Or to elderly women who yearned for a baby? I was neither of those things, and I couldn't imagine what God would want with me.

As if he knew what I was thinking, he told me not to be afraid, and said *again* that God favoured me - I wasn't in trouble. His voice was gentle, and he was so kind it was unnerving.

"You will conceive and give birth to a son. Call him 'God Saves' - Jesus."

My mind blurred over the next details he outlined, because they were all so impossibly big and important: the Son of the Most High, a new king like David - the one promised to rule forever.

The promised one, the anointed Saviour - he would be my son. I was still clutching the broom, I realised. I brought the wood close to my cheek as I took it all in. The wood felt soothing on my skin - something real in this surreal conversation.

Be calm, I thought. I was floating above my body, as though I had become a hero caught up in a famous story. So I would become pregnant and give birth to the Messiah. No big deal. Just keep breathing.

At the back of my mind, there was something troubling me about his words, but I couldn't work out what. I looked out at the olive trees, so still. The wind had completely dropped. Maybe that's what angels did - quieted creation around them. But I could still hear the thudding of my heart.

***

Instantly, I became aware of what was bothering me. Why now? Why hadn't he waited till Joseph and I had moved in together after the wedding and I'd become pregnant? I looked at him questioningly.

Then I realised: it wasn't a future promise. He meant *now*. Before marrying Joseph, I would be pregnant with the Messiah in my womb. I shook my head in confusion. This couldn't be right.

"But how does that work? I - haven't slept with anyone."

Stupid, stupid cheeks. My face felt like it was on fire. I felt like perhaps I was missing something, and I was embarrassed.

(And now my face looked guilty - in front of an angel.)

In the distance I could hear my father singing with his friends, as he walked the path from the fields towards home. I chose not to think about his reaction to all this.

The angel told me that the Holy Spirit, not Joseph, would be the father of the child. I nodded slowly, like I understood what that would mean. (But how? How?)

My father's singing was sounding louder: he was slowly approaching the house.

The angel looked at me again and smiled, as if he could see my question in my eyes. He told me that old Aunt Elizabeth, who nobody thought could ever have children, was already six months pregnant.

This time I nodded with more conviction. Of course - God. I was reasoning as though God were not in the picture, but the Lord had done impossible things ever since he'd breathed the world into being from the chaos of the deep.

The wind made a fierce whisper in the trees, but all other sounds - birds, cicadas and human singing - seemed muffled. The angel took one step back from me, still looking at me, and slowly bowed his head.

"For no word from God will ever fail," he said, his head remaining bowed.

I watched him for a while in wonder, assuming that soon he would disappear from my sight. The sun emerged through the trees, streaming light through the window. The dust motes danced like stars between us.

He looked like one of King Herod's servants, bowing low, yet he was bowing to me. There was an uncomfortable silence while I stood and he bowed. Then it dawned on me as I stared at him: this messenger of heaven, God's mouth on earth, was waiting for my response before he did anything else.

An angel who would normally be waiting with bowed head for God's words, was now waiting with bowed head for mine.

I suddenly had a vision of a whole legion of angels, waiting with the same breathless posture, waiting upon the decision of a teenage girl. I hadn't even realised it was my decision.

Why is God such a team-worker? I was sure the Lord could have found a way to bring the Messiah without involving me. But God had invited people to help change the world since the beginning of time, even though we usually do a pretty poor job of it. I shook my head from thoughts of history and looked out of the window, trying to focus on the spiny branches of the olive tree, the blazing blue of the sky, and to wonder at it all.

I paused just a second while I considered it, but really, the choice was never in doubt. I loved the Lord and trusted Him. Whatever this meant for me, I would do it, because God asked it of me. Why would anyone do otherwise?

I looked back at the angel, trying to catch his eye. I would be like him, I decided. Mirroring his posture, I bowed low.

"I am the Lord's servant," I told him.

The smile he gave was so full of joy, it dazzled me.

He disappeared, and the room at once became darker, though the dust still sparkled.

To reflect on:

"'I am the Lord's servant,' Mary answered. 'May your word to me be fulfilled.' Then the angel left her."

Luke 1:38

For further reading:

Luke 1: 26-38

Over to you:

1. Sometimes we spend ages waiting for something, expecting a certain outcome, only to have our expectations overturned, either in a positive or negative way. To what extent can you relate to that?

2. We often forget Mary was youthful - most likely a teenager. What difference does that make to how you see Mary and the nativity story?

3. 'God as team-worker' - reflect for a while on the paradox of God working with people, even very flawed people, to bring salvation for many. How does that influence how you relate to God?

4. In this retelling, I have put an emphasis on God waiting on Mary, rather than the other way round. What difference does it make to envisage God as one who also waits? What do you make of that idea?

2. Waiting for Reassurance
Mary's Story (Luke 1:39-56)

After the angel left I went to bed as normal, but my mind was racing. I listened to my father's snoring for a long time before I eventually fell asleep; it must have been the middle of the night.

Suddenly, I was outside my home, and all my family had gathered around me in a circle. My parents were right at the front with my brothers and sisters, and clustered around them were cousins, distant aunts, uncles, great-aunts and great-uncles. I hadn't seen most of these faces since the Passover festival when I was five years old and had fallen on Grandpa's walking stick. I had fallen into a huge family reunion, all of them looking at me. I smiled at them and started running to hug them.

But I couldn't run; I could only waddle.

I looked down at my stomach, and it had grown huge - not just like a normal pregnancy, but ten times the size of a watermelon. It seemed to be growing bigger, outwards and forwards, and I pressed my hand on my stomach to try to halt its growth.

I opened my mouth to tell my family about the baby, but there was something wrong - something very, very wrong - and their faces were twisted into hatred. They all took a step back from me, which is when I realised they were encircling me. Then I saw Joseph, who emerged from the crowd with disappointment in his eyes and a large rock in his hands.

I screamed, "No, wait, you don't understand…" but as I looked, they all had rocks, each one of them, and they were raising them above their heads. I sank to my knees and looked up at the sky, but the clouds grew darker and darker.

**

I woke up drenched in sweat. The rest of the night I hardly slept; the dreams kept waking me. The angel had gone, I'd said nothing to my parents, and I was alone with the questions. What would happen to me? There hadn't been anyone in our community killed for adultery for years, decades even, but I had heard talk from other villages where women had been stoned to death. It was written in the law of Moses, after all.

What if... What if they turned against me? What if they didn't understand? I was not ready for all of this. I didn't know how I would protect myself - and the baby - how would I protect the baby?

In the middle of that long night, I started making plans. It was the only thing I could think of doing to stay sane.

As the sky had started to lighten, but before the sun had risen, I ran into Mama's room.

"Uncle Boaz - is he still travelling to the hill country today?"

Mama murmured yes without opening her eyes, still drowsy.

"Is his offer still open?"

This time her eyes sprang open.

"I've changed my mind - I'd like to go along with him after all. I'll go and visit Elizabeth and see how she's doing." I tried to keep my voice casual. "It's been ages since our family paid our respects to theirs. I'm sure she'd appreciate hearing the news about Joseph and me. Can you spare me?"

I have never packed so fast in my life. I wanted to be out of there before they could see that something was wrong.

***

I had held this secret for less than twenty-four hours, and already it was burning a hole in my heart. I was desperate to tell someone. Thank goodness the angel had told me about Elizabeth. I somehow knew that she was the right person to go to with this news. Maybe she could help me.

Do not be afraid. You have found favour with God.

These words kept returning to me, like a mantra. All throughout that endless journey up to the hill country, having to make mind-numbing small talk with my uncle, I was afraid. I tried to push the fear away, but I kept visualising the conversation I would have with my parents, and it never ended well. And Joseph...? I just couldn't even think about Joseph. I would probably blush and look guilty while I told him - there's no way he'd believe me. He was so devout, so upright, and my story sounded so far-fetched.

Really, this was infuriating - the thought of so many people suspecting me of impropriety when I couldn't even talk to a man without going bright red and stammering. It was all so ironic: a devout, unmarried virgin giving birth. I knew how it looked.

You have found favour with God.

God sent his messenger to me, I told myself. He is bigger than this. I knew it didn't look good, but God looks at the heart, not the outward appearance. The Lord knows the truth about me. He'd make it alright. I kept repeating these words to myself, but my heart was drumming in agitation.

The donkeys were slow, and my uncle was telling me about his latest problems with a blight on his crop, but I couldn't follow what he was saying.

How would I do this on my own?

The questions were pouring in now. I tried to think it through calmly, logically. I couldn't exactly expect any help from Joseph, now. I thought sadly of my wedding dreams and the times I had played with a veil with my friends as a young child.

My family loved me, but maybe even they would need to keep their distance. We had a small village, and people were easily offended. We were such a straight-laced community, no scandals. Everyone knew God's law and respected it.

It's not like I had any role models of single motherhood. Although, when I stop to think about it, back in the time of the Judges, Naomi's husband had died and she'd had to look after her sons. Maybe I'd be able to cope, just like she had.

"But even she had Ruth," I thought, and then my eyes brimmed with tears. I felt so alone. Elizabeth was my one hope. I hadn't seen her in so long, and now this journey felt endless. Would she believe me?

My uncle's voice was droning on, and I lost focus. The donkey was rocking me from side to side, and at some point my head dropped to my chest, my eyes closed, and I tumbled in and out of sleep as we journeyed.

***

When I awoke, I could see rolling hills everywhere, and birds were swooping above me. The air was crisper here, and the donkey's tread seemed to echo. I yawned, and wiped my mouth. After the sleep, I felt less anxious. In fact, if I'm perfectly honest, I felt a little foolish.

The thought crept in - what if there had been no angel? What if I had somehow imagined it all? After all, I'd had a very vivid dream last night. Maybe my angel experience was some kind of dream? My body felt no different, and in any case, my period had been late before. Perhaps all the excitement around the betrothal had pushed me over the edge. Maybe there was no baby, and this whole trip was a strange waste of time. Was I going mad?

I didn't know which was the worse option: the thought that I might be supernaturally pregnant, carrying God's chosen Saviour inside me, but destined to be disbelieved by probably everyone I knew; or the thought that I had imagined the whole scenario, when it had all seemed so real and so holy. I was terrified it wasn't true and terrified it was.

But the more awake I became, the more clearly the memory of the angel returned. It definitely felt more real than a dream.

And reality of a different kind was approaching fast. We were rounding the final bend, and to the left, up ahead, with a cluster of houses on the far horizon, Elizabeth's village had just appeared.

I won't tell her straight away, I decided. I'll wait for a little, until I know the right thing to say.

There was something in me that needed to see her for myself. I had experienced the miracle of an encounter with an angel of the Lord, but I also needed to see the supernatural made natural. I needed to see a woman who couldn't possibly be pregnant, miraculously pregnant.

Sometimes we need to see it in someone else before we can believe it for ourselves. When I see Elizabeth, I'll know what to do, I thought to myself.

***

We rounded the track, called the donkeys to a halt and took them to the watering place. Elizabeth had already spotted us and was standing at the door, waving, with a crowd of family behind her. My heart sank. I would have to wait a little while before I had some alone time with her and could whisper my news.

I ran up the path to her and saw that same smile I had always loved, the crows-feet a little deeper around her eyes as she grinned, her hair streaked with grey and white - and her burgeoning stomach. It really was true - God had done the impossible.

We embraced, but almost immediately she stepped back, shocked, one hand to her stomach. I shrank back, fearing that I had done something wrong, but her left hand firmly gripped my shoulder.

Then - and it wasn't like Elizabeth to be loud, but she shouted this out so that everyone could hear:

"But you - you are the guest of honour. I can't believe I'm lucky enough to have you here. You have found favour with God, and you are blessed!

And..." - at this point she looked me right in the eyes - "Blessed is the child you will bear."

I stood there, eyes wide, mouth open. She couldn't have known. There was no way. I could feel my face flushing: my cheeks confirmed the news for her before I could speak.

"You are the mother of my Lord - my womb knows it," she said, and then we were both in tears, hugging, weeping, and everyone crowding round, asking what was going on.

Before I knew what I was doing, I was singing at the top of my lungs. I was so full of relief and praise to God that the song came bursting out of my chest. I couldn't have stopped it if I'd tried. I sang of God's grace and justice, and I poured out praise to a God who cared for the poor and was saving us at last. We were living in miraculous days, and God was with us, and all I could do was sing.

I don't do this kind of thing. Elizabeth doesn't do this kind of thing. We embraced, and I sang, while the others grew hushed and held hands. We were on holy ground, and everyone there knew it.

***

It has been three months now that I've stayed with Elizabeth, ostensibly to help her in her confinement. It has been such a gift. I've needed the calm before facing the others.

Elizabeth has been there for me, quietly trusting that what I say is true, no matter how far-fetched it seems to others. She has held back my hair as I've vomited in the mornings; she's given me ginger and milk and all sorts of helpful tips about pregnancy. Each day we have prayed together all our fears and joys.

It won't be long now - her belly surely can't grow any bigger; she waddles like a duck everywhere she goes. I'll stay for the baby, and then I'll go home, my stomach speaking for me before I have the chance to say anything.

Do not be afraid. You have found favour with God.

After three months of friendship, I am starting to believe it.

To reflect on:

"'As soon as the sound of your greeting reached my ears, the baby in my womb leaped for joy. Blessed is she who has believed that the Lord would fulfil his promises to her!'"

Luke 1:45

For further reading:

Luke 1: 39-56

Over to you:

1. 'Sometimes we need to see it in someone else before we can see it for ourselves.' When have you needed to see the 'supernatural made natural'?

2. Who is a gift in your life? Who are your 'Elizabeths'?

3. When have you ever felt that you're so full of praise for God that it bursts out of you?

4. Mary was called blessed not just for bearing Jesus, but for her belief that the Lord would fulfil his promises to her. How does her belief speak to yours today?

3. Waiting for Mercy
Mary's Story (Matthew 1:18-25)

I had hoped my homecoming would be a quiet thing, so I could break the news to my parents gradually, before the rest of the village found out. No such luck: we arrived mid-afternoon, when everyone was milling around the village square. Mama came out to me, wiping her hands on her apron as she ran, flour-marks on her cheeks. She was talking nineteen to the dozen as she approached, throwing out question after question about how Elizabeth and baby John were doing, but as I jumped down from the donkey and straightened up, my bump gave me away. She stopped, mid-sentence.

It takes a lot to stop my mother talking, but it seems that turning up as a pregnant, unmarried daughter after three months away will do the trick.

She turned to my uncle for explanation, who just shrugged, and took the donkeys off to get the water.

Already a small crowd had gathered, and I saw widow Miriam unsubtly miming a baby-belly to her friends, for the avoidance of all doubt. That meant the whole village would know by tea time.

"Come with me," my mother hissed, putting her arm around me and marching me back home.

"Look, Mama, I can explain," I said, as I tried to keep up with her pace, past the butchers and down to the crossroads. "But can we wait until...?"

I wanted to tell Joseph first. I didn't want him to hear it from someone else. But I had a strange sense that I needed to turn round, so I glanced back just in time to see Joseph, at the other end of the road, lugging a big plank of wood over his shoulder. He stopped, panting, and smiled at me. Then he frowned in confusion. He was probably trying to work out what looked different about me at this distance. I didn't know whether to go on with my mother or turn back to him. The last thing anyone would want would be a confrontation in the street.

Then, as if in slow motion, widow Miriam sidled up to Joseph, whispering in his ear. Joseph looked directly at me, his neck turning purple. He dropped the plank, and walked off at speed.

I sighed, and turned back to my mother.

"Well? Wait until what?" Mama asked.

"Never mind," I said.

***

The next few hours felt long. My mother paced the room; my father was very still and quiet. Initially they asked who had done this to me, and I had to tell them pretty quickly it wasn't Joseph before my usually-placid father walked round to punch him. I told and retold the story of the angel's visit about a million times, but it didn't seem to satisfy them, and they asked who I was protecting.

At one point I felt really faint and asked for some fruit. They could see I turned pale, and rushed to get me some food - and that's when it felt like the turning point. It was as if they suddenly clicked that there was a real baby in there. We ate together in companionable silence, all questions exhausted.

For a while we were silent, and I was just glad to have a break from all the interrogations. Then they asked about Zechariah, and I had to explain that he'd been silent for almost the entire time I'd been there - because he'd seen an angel, and it sounded like the same angel who'd visited me. Their eyes grew wider, and I saw them exchanging meaningful glances, but I couldn't quite work out what they were thinking.

"You can ask Uncle Boaz if you want to check," I said. "He can back me up, at least on that front."

My parents gave each other their annoying secret-code-look that parents do, then Mama nodded, and then looked down.

"Well, we believe you," my father said. "But I'm not sure how many others will."

"That's okay," I said. "I know. I'm just glad you do."

***

The next day felt endless. Mama had determined that I would stay at home and 'keep out of trouble', so I made myself busy. By the afternoon, I was tired. I sat on the steps outside. There was a single cloud, floating across the sky, and it looked so peaceful. I leant my head against the side of the house.

I hated this suspense, wondering what Joseph was thinking and how he would react. He would probably want to divorce me, I had concluded. That's what I told Elizabeth when I was reasoning through what might happen upon my return. She had given me this strange kind of smile, as if she knew better, which drove me mad. She didn't know the future any more than I did, but she said she had this feeling it would turn out okay.

"Yes, but what kind of okay?" I wanted to know. Would I have to be whisked away before people tried to stone me? ("Unlikely," Elizabeth had said. She had known Joseph's family, and they were good people. She didn't think they would want to have me killed.) Divorce was more likely, then.

But her smile had left me with a sliver of completely unrealistic, stubborn hope. If only it could all somehow turn out okay - being married to Joseph, us bringing up the baby together. I was prepared to go it alone, but it would be so much easier in this society with a man's protection. Murmuring a prayer from the Torah, I reminded myself that God would protect me.

But Joseph wasn't here, and there was no word from him. The last time I'd seen him, his face looked decidedly purple. That didn't bode well.

I looked around, trying to distract myself. The land was full of flowers, and I spied some white chamomile. I figured that if I gathered enough to make chamomile tea, Mama might appreciate it. It's not like I had anything else to do. I told my brain not to think about Joseph and the fact that he wasn't here yet. In the middle of a bunch of daisies, I spotted a single blue iris. It looked so beautiful, telling me to hope. I told myself not to give in to easy hope, but I picked it anyway and brought it in.

***

By the time nightfall came, Joseph still hadn't come, and as a family we were decidedly fidgety, squabbling over silly things. It was so hard not knowing what he was going to do.

Just as we were about to give up and get ready for bed, there was a knock on the door. It was him.

Once we were all seated and my mother had offered him (and he had graciously declined) all the food we had in the house, he began.

"Bearing in mind the - ahem - current circumstances," he said, looking anywhere except my stomach, "I thought it wisest to end the betrothal now."

We stared at him in silence. It was hardly unexpected that he would want a divorce, and yet it still felt like a gut-punch. I could suddenly see it all, raising the baby alone, living with my parents - if they'd have me - trying to work in the fields to gather enough to eat each day.

He must have seen our faces, because he shook his head.

"I mean - I want to bring forward the wedding. As soon as possible. Ending the betrothal period early. If you are willing, of course."

My mother was staring at him open-mouthed, as if she couldn't quite believe it. My face was probably looking the same.

He turned to me, though he didn't quite meet my eye.

"I've been busy with the house today, to make it ready," he said. "It's a bit rough around the edges, but I can keep working on it."

The room exploded with movement and sound. My mother was kissing Joseph repeatedly, my father making loud pronouncements of excitement. Joseph, trapped in the middle of their exuberant affection, looked positively scared. I shot them a look to back off him a bit, but I don't think they noticed. Papa went to fetch the best wine, and Mama left to make some almond and orange cake, even at this late hour. It was time for celebration.

Joseph and I were left alone for a moment, sitting awkwardly across from one another. He twirled his hair around his finger and looked at the floor. I tried to take it all in: the Lord was protecting me. He was looking after the baby. This was so much more than I'd imagined or dared hope for.

"Thank you," I said, still not looking quite at him.

"I thought I'd name him," he said. My heart leapt - this meant he would be formally adopting him. I just couldn't believe how okay he was about all this. I knew he was a good guy before, but this had really surprised me.

But - oh! - the angel had told me he should be called Jesus. What if he picked the wrong name?

"His name will be..." and then he said "Jesus," just as I ventured, "Jesus?"

We stared at each other, then burst out laughing.

"How did you...?" I asked him.

"An angel told me," he said.

"Me, too."

We looked at each other. I could see the wonder in his eyes, too, and I felt that same thrill again of the Spirit that I'd felt when I saw Elizabeth.

The words of my own song came back to me, "His mercy extends to those who fear him." That's what I felt then: the sheer mercy of the Lord. I opened my mouth to say something to Joseph - and then Mama came back in with the food, already talking animatedly about the invitation list. I closed my mouth again and smiled. I stored the moment up in my heart.

To reflect on:

"His mercy extends to those who fear him,
from generation to generation."

Luke 1:50 (from Mary's song)

For further reading:

Matthew 1:18-25

Over to you:

1. Mary was not the only one who faced rejection and social ridicule for bearing the Messiah: Joseph also laid himself open to that rejection by society. Just as Isaiah had faced ridicule for trusting in God when others made decisions by more worldly values, Joseph chose to believe the word of God about the situation rather than how it looked to others. In what situations in your life do you need to heed the word of God rather than how it appears to the world?

2. "His mercy extends to those who fear him" - spend some time thinking about the mercy of God, which Luke defines as rescuing those who are suffering or in deep need. How does this verse comfort, unsettle or excite you? To whom can you show mercy today?

4. Waiting to Arrive
Mary's Story (Luke 2:1-7)

The census couldn't have come at a worse time. Mama went pale when she heard - she'd been calling me 'goose' for days, because of the way I was waddling. I thought that my stomach couldn't get any bigger. It was strange to look down and not see my toes anymore.

We thought at first that it might just be Joseph who would have to register but of course, because I was officially now his 'wife', I would have to go, too. This sent my mother off into an impromptu long, loud cursing-prayer for deliverance from the Roman oppressors, and it was hard to make any sensible plans.

We delayed and procrastinated, hoping that maybe the baby would come before we had to go, but in the end, Joseph and I decided to do the impossible: we would cart my mammoth belly up to Bethlehem by donkey.

It was usually a three-day journey, but we knew that we would need to go more slowly. If you happen to know any pregnant women, tell them I would not recommend doing a journey by donkey. Or at all, for that matter. At first it was easier, because others were journeying with us, and they were generous with their water and other provisions. Then they all overtook us, and we were left doing the journey alone.

On the third day, we were still not even near Jerusalem. Some parts of the road were deserted, but we never knew what lay behind each bush, and we were very aware we had no protection. We didn't have money for an inn, so we headed to a town each day and asked for people's hospitality.

Back at home, we had often given shelter and food to any travellers coming through, and willingly, too, but there is something humbling about being dependent on others for what you usually provide yourself. Each time someone welcomed us into their home I would want to cry with gratitude. Right at the time when I wanted to be feeling in control, like a person about to be looking after a very important baby should feel, I was completely helpless and dependent on the kindness and mercy of others.

***

The hills rolled on for miles, so we were going slowly uphill, then slowly downhill again, trying to minimise each bump. That's when the pain started. Elizabeth had warned me that I might have preparatory pains before labour, and I told myself that's what they were. I didn't want to worry Joseph, so I just went quiet, but I think he knew something was up - he slowed the donkey right down. The pains lifted after a few hours, and I was relieved. But already I was dreading the return journey and wondering how I would do it.

When we passed Jerusalem, I was torn. On the one hand, I was exhausted, every bone in my body was screaming with pain, and I kept feeling faint, desperate to reach Bethlehem. On the other hand, we were tantalisingly near to the beautiful temple. Perhaps we could have stopped off, seen around the great city, even worshipped there. Jerusalem was the greatest of cities, and I wanted to worship in God's dwelling place.

I may have even suggested this to Joseph, who just raised his eyebrows in response, as if to say, 'Why are you thinking about tourism at a time like this?' which was a fair enough point, and we went on.

The next day, the cramps were coming every few minutes.

I shouldn't have come, I thought. We should have just defied the Romans and stayed at home. That is where I should have been giving birth - with my family around me. My eyes filled with tears. I tried not to focus on those thoughts and instead looked at the flies buzzing round the donkey's ears. I tried to sing a line from my song, "the Mighty One has done great things for me - holy is his name", but I was panting for breath, and it was hard to focus on anything other than the pain.

***

We reached Bethlehem at nightfall. The crowds were ridiculous, as though the entire country had been squeezed into this one little town. I began to feel claustrophobic; the cramps were coming more quickly and the pain was all-consuming. The noise, the shouting, the pushing, it all became too much. I kept myself on the donkey, but my strength was fading. I was desperate - desperate - for somewhere to lie down.

I was done: even at that stage I felt like I'd reached the end of myself. I wanted to click my fingers and be back at home with my mother in our lovely house in Nazareth, with the fire blazing in the courtyard; not in this seething pit of chaos.

Joseph looked at me: I could no longer speak, and tears were falling down my cheeks with a tired regularity. That's when he kicked into another gear: he started shouting and pushing through the crowds, not seeming to care whether he was offending a peasant or a Roman official. Usually, I would have been mortified to be causing so much fuss, but this time I was just faintly grateful, only half aware of what was going on around me.

Joseph somehow got us registered, then we went to find the room for the night. "It's my great-aunt's house," he murmured to me, as we pushed through the crowds. I heard him, but I couldn't reply. Soon, I thought, soon we will be there and we will be looked after, and I can concentrate on having this baby.

We reached the house, but by now it was pitch black. I was glad Joseph knew Bethlehem so well from his childhood; I had no idea where we were.

"We'll get you warm and comfortable really soon," Joseph promised, but his forehead was engraved with worry lines. He rapped on the door once, then again, with more urgency. He was pounding on it a third time when an elderly woman came to the door, holding a lantern. She opened the door a small way.

"It's Joseph," he told her. "I'm sorry it's so late, but we've been travelling for a long time and we really need to come in."

He pushed on the door, but she held it firmly in place.

"Sorry, we're full. You've seen what the town is like today. I'd like to welcome you, but I just can't. You'll have to find somewhere else. The guest room is crammed with family already, and there are eight Roman soldiers who are currently helping themselves to our wine."

She made to shut the door, but Joseph wedged it open with his foot.

"But - you don't understand. My wife is about to have a baby. I mean, literally about to have a baby. She's in labour right now."

Her eyes narrowed.

"And whose baby is it?" she said, raising her eyebrows.

Joseph stepped back.

"What do you mean?" he said.

"What I mean is," she said, and here she looked pointedly at me, "this is a God-fearing family, and we don't want any shame brought upon our doorstep. We're not stupid. We can count."

"But - please...?" begged Joseph.

"I'm sorry, but that's how it is." Though she didn't open the door any further, she was now looking at the floor. "Anyway, it's for the best for you. This is not a private affair. Everyone is here."

Her voice contained a hint of threat.

"It's not just me. You know what I'm saying? I'm sorry, but that's the way it is."

The door shut, the donkey brayed, and I cried out in pain as the cramps intensified. They were coming every few seconds now, and tears streamed down my face.

Far from home, I had just been rejected by the people I hoped would welcome us. I felt humiliated, angry and desperate, all at the same time. I tried to remember the line of my song about scattering the proud and feeding the hungry, but I was panicking.

"I want my Mama!" I sobbed at my point of weakness, because I was scared and didn't know what to do.

To reflect on:

"He has performed mighty deeds with his arm;
he has scattered those who are proud in their inmost thoughts.
He has brought down rulers from their thrones
but has lifted up the humble.
He has filled the hungry with good things
but has sent the rich away empty."

Luke 1:51-53 (from Mary's song)

For further reading:

Luke 2:1-7

Over to you:

1. Jesus was born in Bethlehem, seemingly by accident. It was down to the timing of an inconvenient Roman census that forced Joseph and Mary to leave their home of Nazareth. But Matthew sees in it a greater plan, foretold by the prophets, that confirms that the baby born would be a ruler like David, but even greater than him. Can you think of a time in your life when it seemed like a disaster, but in retrospect you can see how God worked through it?

2. In the midst of the birth, it must have seemed to Mary like this would be the last thing that God would have wanted for his son. But Jesus' birth, laid out in an animal's feeding trough, meant that he identified with homeless, despised or rejected people. In her book, *Wearing God*, Lauren Winner points out that we often envisage God via a few well-worn biblical metaphors: shepherd, king, light.[13] But how does it expand our sense of who God is when

---

[13] Lauren Winner, *Wearing God*, HarperOne, 2015

we see him as a homeless person? And with this reminder of Jesus' birth, how does that influence the way that we respond to homeless people and refugees?

3. Mary's song declares that Jesus' birth will herald the great reversal of the status quo. The proud who are high on their thrones will be brought low; the humble will be lifted up. Mary and Joseph, symbolic of the world's poor, were sent away to Bethlehem, while Roman soldiers had the power to take over someone's home. But in Mary's prophecy, God gives good things to the hungry and sends the rich away empty. To what extent do we need to realign our view of society with Mary's and God's eyes?

5. Waiting for the Pain to Stop
Mary's Story (Luke 2:7, Romans 8:18-26)

Joseph paced once towards the door of the house, then turned back again. I had collapsed onto the donkey's neck, its rough hair beneath my cheeks. I could no longer lift my body up.

"It's okay," he said. "I know a place. It'll be okay."

He guided me a little way down the road, heading out of the village, to a cave carved out of rock.

"It belongs to our family. We used to keep all sorts of animals, but now there are mainly just donkeys for transport. It will be dry, at least, and we can sort things out tomorrow."

I nodded. Given the alternative of giving birth while sitting astride a donkey, it seemed like a palace. Joseph helped me down from the donkey and started emptying our bags of the clothes we had brought.

"Here," he said, "rest here a while."

I settled myself down. It felt so good to be lying down. Right at that moment, I vowed never again to go on a donkey. I would just have to lie here in this cave forever.

Joseph made to leave.

"Don't go," I whimpered.

"I'll be back in one hundred seconds," he said. "Count them, and I'll be back."

In the dark, I started to count to one hundred.

One, two, three…

I'm really going to have this baby, I thought to myself. Pregnancy is strange. In my fifth month, the sickness had gone, and I still had lots of energy. I had kept forgetting I was pregnant, and then the baby kicked, and I would laugh in surprise -

The pain stopped me mid-thought. I breathed. I counted.

There was no forgetting now that I was pregnant.

Now that I didn't have to worry about staying on the donkey, I was more conscious of what my body was feeling. What I discovered was that my body really, really hurt. This was worse than when I jumped off the roof of my house at the age of four, believing I could fly. I breathed deeply, and went back to counting.

Thirty-nine, forty, forty-one…

The contraction subsided, and I lay back on the clothes for a bit. There was a vague smell of animal urine in the air, and I felt stomach acid touching my throat. I will not vomit, I told myself. I told my stomach acid to stay where it was. Where was Joseph? Another contraction came on me, and I heard a sound around the cave, like a cow mooing deeply. For a moment, I was confused: there were only donkeys in the cave as far as I knew - where had the cow come from? It took me a while to realise that sound was coming from me. I had no idea I could groan that deeply.

Seventy-two, seventy-three, seventy-four…

I can't do this. I have to do this, but I can't.

The pain was overwhelming. I was not ready for this. All these months I thought I was ready and prepared, but now I wanted to turn the clock back. It felt like a boa constrictor was wrapping itself round my back and stomach and hips, squeezing and squeezing.

"Make it stop!" I yelled, and my voice echoed all around the cave. I was all alone. Who exactly was I asking to make it stop?

God. Though I was alone, God was still there.

"Please, God, make the pain stop," I whimpered. I didn't know whether I was supposed to pray that or not, but I did. The smell of animals and mould hit me again, and this time I vomited.

One hundred, one hundred and one…

Joseph still wasn't back. It wasn't supposed to be like this. I recalled the image of the angel. Surely this couldn't have been what God meant to happen? Maybe if I had been at home and not spent the last week on a donkey it might have been better. How could I give birth here, in this dank, dark place? I couldn't even see my hand in front of my face. I was supposed to be taking care of this special, chosen baby. Had I already failed?

It was wrong, everything was wrong. The pain came upon me again. I wished for water, but couldn't move.

One hundred and sixty-six…

Joseph was still not here. Suddenly, the thought came to me: I'm going to die here. My strength had gone, but the pain continued, and I could feel myself fading. I was shivering uncontrollably, my teeth chattering. I thought of my great-grandmother and how I had watched her die. Though she was old, she had been fit, and in my childhood brain I thought she would be immortal. She got sick, and in the end she stopped eating. It wasn't that she wanted to die; I think she just wanted the pain to end, and she somehow knew it was her time. Just then, I had that sense, too.

I was going to die. I accepted my fate calmly. I was too tired to do otherwise.

Two hundred and eighty-four, two hundred and eighty-five...

Now I felt like I was floating above my body, watching myself from above. Unexpectedly, I heard a voice singing. It was my own voice, like a memory from long ago.

"My soul glorifies the Lord and my spirit rejoices in God my Saviour."

How could it be my voice? I was too tired to work it out. Maybe I was really singing aloud; maybe it was just in my head. My breathing slowed, and I listened to the words:

"For the Mighty One has done great things for me - holy is his name."

The Lord had done great things for me - already I had seen those great things. They flashed into my mind: the angel bowing; Elizabeth hugging me; Joseph wanting to marry me. I didn't know if it was my life flashing before my eyes or something else, but a great peace washed over me. It would be okay. I didn't know exactly what would be okay, but it would be okay. I breathed deeply again.

Four-hundred and sixteen, four hundred and seventeen...

I might have blanked out for a minute. I wasn't sure what number I was counting anymore, but I continued anyway. I knew I was waiting for something - for the pain to stop, somehow, or for it to stop being so dark - I couldn't remember. I kept counting.

Eight hundred and four, eight hundred and five...

I opened my eyes. It was still black, but I felt different. My body was telling me to push. In a rush, it all came back to me - I was going to give birth to the boy who would become God's anointed Saviour. And I was alone.

I could feel the weight of his head bearing down and I began to push and moan at the same time.

"Jo-seph!" I prayed fervently that he would appear.

As if on cue, when I had reached eight hundred and ninety Joseph entered the cave, walking quickly but carefully, carrying a knife, a bowlful of water, blankets and a lamp.

"If they're not going to welcome us, they can at least supply us," he muttered, and I smiled gratefully.

I saw on his face the moment he realised he would be delivering a baby alone. He gave a pale smile.

The seconds blurred into minutes; endless time, no time at all. Then all at once, the miracle: my voice was not the only one crying. A miniature roar came from Joseph's arms, and we laughed hysterically, crying with joy.

Joseph wiped him clean and brought him to me; I snuggled him close to my body.

"My soul glorifies the Lord," I sang, with a croaky and cracked throat, "And my spirit rejoices in God my Saviour."

I stroked his head tenderly; so soft, so vulnerable. This was the moment humanity had been waiting for: the Saviour appearing, wrinkled and new.

I kissed him as gently as I could, tears of awe running down my cheeks.

"Hello, Jesus," I said. "It's so good to see you."

To reflect on:

"I consider that our present sufferings are not worth comparing with the glory that will be revealed in us."

Romans 8:18

For further reading:

Luke 2:7, Romans 8:18-26

Over to you:

1. Paul compares the Christian life as being in the pains of childbirth (Romans 8) - we are groaning as we wait for heaven. When have you felt like how I imagined Mary in labour - crying out to God to stop the pain, forgetting the purpose of the pain, longing to see the face of the Saviour?

2. To what extent do you find the image of labour helpful in expressing the pain and suffering of the world?

6. General Reflections
Mary's Story

As you look back through Mary's story:

1. Which parts came to life for you in a new way?

2. Which parts most resonated with your experience?

3. Which parts challenged, troubled or encouraged you?

4. Which aspects of God's character did you glimpse in Mary's story?

5. Which verses would you want to memorise or meditate on further?

1 Peter describes our state as Christians as 'exiles and foreigners'[14] - our home is heaven. As far back as Sarah and Abraham, our spiritual ancestors were nomads, wanderers in the wilderness; our Saviour was a homeless drifter, born in an emergency shelter. We are not home yet: heaven is our true home.

- ~ **Sarah and Abraham** were on the outskirts of society, with Sarah in disgrace for most of her life for being childless.
- ~ **Isaiah** spoke against the status quo, which made him unpopular.
- ~ **John** spent his life in the desert or in prison, away from the centre of civilisation.
- ~ **Mary** lived with a question mark of propriety over her life and morals, despite being utterly obedient to God and honoured by God.

6. How does their disgrace and isolation speak into our situations, either generally as Christians, or those who are waiting?

---

[14] 1 Pet 1:1, 2:11

Music

Listen to a version of The Magnificat (Mary's song, 'My soul magnifies the Lord…'). Classical recordings abound: for longer pieces try Vivaldi, CPE Bach, JC Bach, or Rutter; for more contemporary pieces try My Soul Magnifies by Helen Dennis. As you listen to Mary's song of thanksgiving, consider the ways you have been included by God. Give thanks for 'Elizabeths' in your life who encourage you.

Creative Exercise: Prayer Posture

Think of the impossible things God is asking of you at this moment. Imagine yourself into the story as Mary facing the angel. As you bring all these burdens to God in prayer, take a bowing posture and try saying, "I am the Lord's servant". Listen to what God says to you.

Then try a different posture, as you imagine Mary would have when she saw Elizabeth. Think through all that God is asking of you, and say, "My soul glorifies the Lord". Listen to what God says to you.

How do the two postures help you in prayer?

Heart-cry Prayer

Oh, Lord. I have been alone in this too long. I am tired of feeling left behind, like my life is on pause while the world whirls around me. I am tired of trying to think positively when my life yawns before me, bland and dull. Won't you please release me from feeling so stuck? Or maybe give me someone to be with me in this, to support me. Or give me something fresh, some nugget of hope. I have been crying to you so long. I know you hear me, God. But I need to know you hear me. Won't you please stop the loneliness? Amen.

Benediction

For all who think no one notices them,
For all who feel forgotten by friends and God;
May you know the fiery love
Of the God who overturns tables in the temple,
Who disturbs the comfortable and defends the helpless.

May the Holy Spirit come upon you
With tears, joy and a blanket of peace;
So you may know once again in your heart
The weighty comfort of God's presence with you.

May you who live out your life
In unseen, unremarkable faithfulness
Know the remarkable favour of the Lord upon you.
May you glimpse how dearly beloved you are
Among the saints of God.

For all who dread the next day's dreariness,
May we lift our eyes up once again;
May we fix our eyes on the Author and Perfecter of our faith,
With fresh wonder.
Amen.

Some of these reflections and exercises are repeated in the Group Bible Study.

SECTION FIVE
The God Who Waits

1. Epilogue: The God Who Waits

This is where we started:

Everyone is waiting, and everyone hates it.

We hate waiting, because we want to know the end of the story, and we want that ending to be good.

Leaning into Discomfort, Finding God There

In all of our little and bigger waits in life, we are participating in the longest wait of history: for the return of Christ, the heralding of heaven and all evil to be undone. We have eternity etched in our souls, and we yearn for it.

Sometimes, like Mary and Sarah, we get to experience that 'goodness of the Lord in the land of the living'.[15] We should celebrate the happy endings whenever they occur. It is a joy when God grants us the desires of our hearts.

For others of us, we are still waiting after decades, and it's hard.

This book does not offer straightforward solutions to the struggles of waiting. Nor is there a list of action points so it feels less like waiting and more like doing. I don't offer these, because I don't see them in these Bible stories. The Bible does not disguise the discomfort of waiting. Instead, I see people who battled through difficult times and prevailed. I see people who trusted, doubted, despaired - and trusted again.

So often, as Christians, we rush to solutions to ease the discomfort, but these stories invite us to be honest about the wrestling. This is the paradox: when we run away from the tension of waiting, it comes back twice as hard. But when we lean into the discomfort, we find God there.

The following aren't so much solutions as they are footholds of comfort and perspective as we wait.

---

[15] Psalm 27:13

Emotions are to be felt, not squashed

It is always my intention in writing to describe truly what *is* - for only then can we picture what *could be*. Likewise, when we are told to focus on how we 'should' behave, it can often block us from healthily processing that emotion. If you've ever tried telling someone who's angry that they shouldn't be angry, you will know what I'm talking about.

When we picture Bible characters or 'good Christians' in a period of waiting, so often what we have in mind is a stoic approach to life - enduring difficulty without complaint. But this is not how Bible heroes waited. We need the Hebrew psalms that rage and wrestle, and we need these stories. These characters, represented in the Advent candle wreath, struggled and questioned as much as we do. This gives us breathing room to be like the saints who've gone before us.

It gives us space to wait in quiet trust, or to wait with doubt and questions, and know that either way we are deeply loved by God.

God Shows Up

God acted to rescue Sarah and spoke to reaffirm the promise to her. Isaiah's calling was such a profound and literally earth-shaking experience that it sustained him through his frustrating ministry. Jesus spoke words of truth and comfort to John the Baptist when he most needed it. God gave Mary Elizabeth, so she would have a friend and companion to walk with as she processed her calling.

In the Bible, as in our own lives, God often shows up 'late'. The wait for God feels agonisingly long, and there is still a question of why God didn't come sooner. God shows up late, but not *too late*. We can open ourselves to the possibility of God speaking to us in and through our waiting.

Through Waiting, We Get a Little Hungrier for God and Heaven

Deuteronomy 8 references the Israelites' time wandering the desert for years and says, "[the Lord] humbled you, causing you to hunger and then feeding you with manna" (Deut 8:3). If we have enough money and power (which includes most of us in the Western world), we do not have to wait for much. We may not know daily the literal hunger of having to wait for our food before it's provided. We forget how dependent we are until our privilege is stripped from us. In a similar way, when we are forced to wait for something good, it increases our appetite for God.

This is not to say that God is a cruel parent, letting children starve before satisfying them. Rather, it is saying something a little more complex: in this broken world, waiting is inevitable, though not equally distributed. When we're in situations out of our control, we can choose to listen to our exposed desires and find theological truths there.

It causes us to realise that we are not ultimately in control of our lives and we appeal to God as a compassionate ruler. When there is a delay for justice, we cry out to God simply because we know there should be justice. When there is a delay of goodness, we cry out to God because we know God is kind and merciful and there should be goodness in the world. It is the good nature of God that makes waiting such a frustration and a mystery. Yet entering into that waiting has the power to mature us spiritually.

With a period of waiting, our spiritual senses sharpen and our priorities are clearer. We hunger for good, but beyond that, we hunger for God. A season of waiting, even when it feels agonisingly, cruelly long, is an opportunity to look beyond our longings to our hunger and thirst for God.

The Participation is the Purpose

We wonder what the purpose of waiting is when we can't clearly see any inner transformation or outer benefit. But when it comes to waiting, *the participation is the purpose*. Whenever we wait in little ways we ache a little, and with that ache we participate in the greater wait for Christ to return. The participation doesn't just lead us to the purpose of waiting: the participation is the purpose.

Underscoring our desire for a better life and an end to uncertainty is the truest desire of all: a return to paradise, naked and unafraid, walking in creation with God, in perfect harmony. Our souls are homesick for this, and it does us good to remember.

Whenever we long for something greater than this life offers us, we become more aware, not less aware, of reality. The life we live right now is beautiful, but it's a dull greyscale compared to the technicolour of what lies before us.

You Are Not Forgotten

The Bible text condenses the periods of waiting, but we need to remember the silences and gaps. Our lives are not all action and declaration; they are often made up of quiet, undramatic faithfulness. Our lives are often boring. We see how God cared for the people who waited. Even when God is silent, we are not forgotten or abandoned.

Sometimes Waiting is a Mercy

In Isaiah's day, God's delay of war and judgement in Judah was an act of mercy. There are times in our lives where the wait feels agonising. Yet when we look back, we see the grace of God in that delay, and we are glad for it. Perhaps it saved us from a poor decision; perhaps it changed our direction for the better. There are occasions when we can attest to the transformation of our character or other disguised blessings that have accompanied a season of waiting. Consider times in your lives when you have been ultimately glad for what seemed at the time like a meaningless delay. It pays to watch out for these where they happen - God's goodness can often be found in unexpected places.

God Waits With Us

Everyone is waiting, and everyone finds it uncomfortable. But in Paul's letter to the Romans, we read something remarkable: God also is waiting, and also finds it uncomfortable.

> "I consider that our present sufferings are not worth comparing with the glory that will be revealed in us. For the creation waits in eager expectation for the children of God to be revealed...
> "We know that the whole creation has been groaning as in the pains of childbirth right up to the present time.
> "Not only so, but we ourselves, who have the first fruits of the Spirit, groan inwardly as we wait eagerly for adoption to sonship, the redemption of our bodies...
> "In the same way, the Spirit helps us in our weakness. We do not know what we ought to pray for, but the Spirit himself intercedes for us through wordless groans."
>
> Romans 8: 18-19, 22-23, 26

As we wait, creation groans with us. Christian brothers and sisters groan with us. Extraordinarily, God the Holy Spirit also groans with us, feeling our pain and giving it expression in heaven's courts even when we can't.

The Bible shows a God who is not distant, but engaged. Whenever God acts, God threads that story into ordinary people's lives. Whenever we groan with waiting we can know God is groaning with us, even as God plans our relief.

And this is the truth driving this book - that when we wait, God is in the waiting.

It means it's not an accident, it's not a mistake, it's not a cruel prank. God has not taken a long nap. The time is not wasted. God is present with us. It's not much, but it's also everything.

The Longest Wait: Christ Will Come Again

If I'm honest, I don't tend to think much about Jesus' return. Sometimes if I'm feeling morose I might think about my own death and meeting him in that way, but I don't think about him coming back to earth to wrap up history. It's one of those doctrines that the church doesn't tend to talk about very much. People wearing sandwich boards warning that Christ will come again tend to be ridiculed rather than revered.

After all, it's a little embarrassing: the church has been saying it will happen for 2000 years, but it hasn't happened (yet). We know we will meet Christ when we die, and we are familiar with death, but it is harder to anticipate Christ's return because it is the end of everything as we know it. At some point, after 2000 years of expecting Christ to turn up at any second, the church has grown complacent. It is an act of faith even to ponder the doctrine.

The other reason we don't think much about Christ's return is because it's hard to wait. Our world - and even our churches - value people of action, those with full diaries and lots of achievements. To be told simply to wait is a frustratingly passive command. It's counter-intuitive. Jesus told his followers to be ready for his return, but it's difficult to exist in a state of perpetual expectation. It's like trying to keep your eyes open all night when your body is telling you to sleep.

We tend to think of living in expectation of Christ's return as though we were in an airport departure lounge: bored and running out of snacks; watching the lights flicker and change on the arrivals board, hoping for some indication that he will come. But waiting for Christ is not something that we do as a separate activity; rather, we wait for Christ as we go about our lives.

Waiting for Christ's return is not an airport lounge. It's a very long third trimester.

Waiting for Christ as Pregnancy

When I was pregnant, there was a brief window in the middle of my pregnancy in which I could eat Chinese food again without feeling nauseous (impossible in the first trimester), and I could get off a sofa without having to do it in three stages (impossible in the third trimester). In that golden middle stage, it was easy to forget that I was expecting a baby. I lived my life as normal, and only when I looked in the mirror at my changed silhouette or felt the fluttering in my womb from the baby's kicks did I remember that I was waiting for a baby to be born.

Like Jesus' forebears, who longed for his coming on earth, we long for his return.

Except that we don't long for it, not every day.

Most days we just long for a better version of this life.

It is hard to remember that one day Jesus will return, and this world will be unwrapped to reveal a new heaven and earth. For the most part we go through our daily lives as normal, because we cannot hold too much wonder in our hands at once.

Recalling the doctrine of Christ's return and our own mortality, particularly if we're feeling happy and comfortable in this life, may give us an uncomfortable twinge of pain, reminding us of what's coming.

The doctrine of Christ's return is therefore unsettling. It reminds us of the challenge to not become too comfortable here among the cinnamon treats, twinkly lights and saccharine music.

As we remember Christ's first coming as a wanderer, a refugee in his infancy, we remember also that we are merely travelling through this world. Though we may have put down roots in good lives, we are not home yet.

Waiting for Christ as Labour

"We know that the whole creation has been groaning as in the pains of childbirth right up to the present time." Romans 8:22

Others of us feel differently about life: not merely pregnant, but in labour. We have been in pain for so long that we can't remember a reality without it. We know the agony of waiting. We can't remember the purpose of the pain or what it is we're waiting for; all we can do is cry out for relief and feel despair when the pain continues.

We groan, wordlessly; but sometimes we sense God the Holy Spirit groaning alongside us, and it helps, a little.

Sometimes we experience the companionship of Christ, who entered the world with a cry, and left it with a cry of pain, and we know him truly as 'God with us', Immanuel.

Sometimes we have a sense of these truths, and it is like a blessed pain-killer; other times it is not enough, and we are left floundering, gasping for breath, wondering how we shall continue.

For those of us who endure the labour-pains of physical suffering or heartache, the doctrine of Christ's second coming sounds like comfort. This will end. The darkness feels everlasting and all-powerful, but it does not have the final say. It is temporary: God is eternal. We already know the ending of the story, and that ending is good.

***

When I was in the pushing stage of labour, it took all my energy just to draw the next breath. I had almost forgotten there was a baby at the end of the pain. Sometimes life is like that. There's no energy for anything other than surviving, and you forget what life is supposed to be all about. You forget that Christ will return, or that there is a deeper, more beautiful life beyond this one.

Eventually, he arrived, my little baby, and they brought him to me. I hadn't met him before, and yet I knew him. His face was simultaneously new and familiar.

I have a confession: I am not one of those people who thinks all babies are beautiful. I think most are plain ugly, if I'm totally honest, and I find myself wincing at the red and crumpled newborns, inventing suitable compliments for the sake of the parents. (Not yours. Your baby is genuinely beautiful.) While my husband and I are alright-looking, let's just say I was more convinced of our progeny's genetic tendency towards brains rather than beauty.

But then they handed him to me, and I was unprepared for how perfect, how gorgeous he looked to me. I was genuinely surprised. My first words to him were, "But he's so beautiful!" At that moment of seeing how beautiful he was, despite the pain and exhaustion, I felt a deep contentment, as though I knew everything would be alright.

I reckon that's how it will be. Christ will come again, and we will see that face for the first time, and it will be strangely familiar. More clearly than ever before, we will see the all-surpassing love; the burning heart of justice and holiness; the gentleness and compassion, power and glory of the God who made, knows and loves us. Then will we live as we were created to live - with no more sickness, suffering, sin, isolation or desolation. This is the moment we are all waiting for, with every breath we take. And we will say, "But he's so beautiful!" and we will know that now, at last, everything really will be alright.

This is my prayer for us all: that in all our waiting, big and small, short and long, we would see glimpses of the beauty of Christ and long to know him more.

2. A Benediction for Those Who Wait

God, the Holy Spirit,
Who groans with us,
Thank you that you do not leave us unsupported.
Help us to know we're not alone.

Be with us when we have no words to pray,
No strength to endure,
And no one by our side.

Take up that weight we carry;
Fill us with the knowledge of your presence,
And be the best friend at our side, we pray.

Dear Lord, be with us in the waiting.

Lord Jesus Christ
May we know you afresh in our lives,
Celebrate your first coming
And long for your return.

In our uncertainty,
May we remember that we already know the end of the story,
And the ending is good.
Breathe hope in our hearts and strength to our bones.

Dear Lord, be with us in the waiting.

Loving Heavenly Parent - Father and Mother of all,
You have been waiting since the beginning of time;
Help us in the uncertainty; the doubt, despair and frustration;
Be at our side as we walk upon invisible paths,
And write upon our hearts that you are for us, not against us,
And that nothing can separate us from your love.

Dear Lord, be with us in the waiting.

We look to the beginning - at the perfect world you created;
We look to the middle - where you entered our world with us, as dust;
We look to the end - where you will restore all things.
Lord Jesus,
As we wander through our lives,
Won't you please turn our heads to the beginning and end;
And embrace us, honour us, sustain us
As we live in the in-between.

Lord Jesus,
Who waited for centuries in the light of heaven,
Nine months in the warm darkness of a womb,
And three days in a tomb -

Be with us in the waiting, we pray.

Amen.

3. A Benediction for Times of Advent

For those whose life has been stuck on pause,
May you know the comfort and presence
Of the God who waits with us.

Come, Lord Jesus, as we wait for you

May we whose darkness feels everlasting
Remember that pure light has entered the world,
And the darkness has not overpowered it.

Come, Lord Jesus, as we wait for you

May we see Christ, the despised one;
Christ, who loved the outsider,
Who tasted bitterness and endured death;
May he comfort us in our distress
And disturb us in our comfort.

Come, Lord Jesus, as we wait for you

When all we experience is endless waiting and fruitlessness,
Give us the strength to look up and forward to you.
May we long for the taste of heaven,
Our true and future home.

Come, Lord Jesus, as we wait for you

May we who carry weariness and pain
Receive sustenance from a Saviour
Who entered and exited the world with a cry of distress.

Come, Lord Jesus, as we wait for you

May we who have grown too comfortable
Among the twinkly lights of this world
See afresh the true and glorious light of Christ.

Come, Lord Jesus, as we wait for you

As we remember the great cloud of witnesses
Who waited in faith for your coming on earth -
Sarah and Abraham and the patriarchs;
Isaiah and the prophets;
Zechariah, Elizabeth and John;
Joseph and Mary,
And all those unnamed saints who cried out for salvation -
May we join our voice with theirs, and pray:
Maranatha. Come, Lord Jesus.
Come, Lord Jesus.
Come.

4. Summary and Reflections
Those Who Wait

Reflection Questions:

1. Which character most resonated with you? Why is this?

2. As you think over these stories, what most surprised you?

3. How have these stories taught you about waiting?

4. In which ways have you encountered God through this book?

The Clock

Revisit the picture of the clock, and consider all those areas of your life in which you feel 'liminal': in-between, unfulfilled, in limbo.

~   Over the past few weeks, as you've spent time sitting with the discomfort of waiting, what have you discovered through this practice?
~   In what ways, if any, has your approach to waiting changed?
~   Which prayers, if any, have been answered?
~   Overall, what have you gained from this journey?

A prayer of surrender

Wrestling with God is tiring. The idea with this prayer is to represent with your body an prayerful attitude of surrender.

~ If you are in a position to do so, move your body into whatever feels most naturally a position of surrender to God; perhaps sitting with hands upraised, or lying on the floor, or kneeling low.

~ Breathe deeply as you do so and spend some time there.

~ One by one, bring the hopes unfulfilled to God, perhaps symbolising this by clenching and unclenching your hands. How does it feel to say, "I surrender this into your hands", or "I entrust this into your hands"?

~ If you like the song "All to Jesus I surrender", this might be a good one to sing or play in the background.

Music

'I surrender all - All to Jesus' - there's a simple recording by Robin Mark of this hymn or a one-verse acoustic version by Libbi. (Casting Crowns do a modern tune.) Play the song or read aloud the lyrics, and these words as a prayer for your own life.

Heart-cry Prayer

This is about emotional honesty in prayer when you don't have the words to pray - giving voice to the deepest disappointments so you can bring them to God. (It's probably less embarrassing if you do it alone.)

~ Breathe deeply, and slow down your breathing.

~ As you think of each area of your life where there is frustration, confusion or hopes deferred, groan to God. Without words, we join with the Spirit's groaning. Let that groan be a wordless prayer to God for his salvation and wholeness to come to this broken world.

Suffering and the Gift of Heaven - a Christmas activity

~ On a large piece of paper, doodle on the theme of suffering and longing - thinking about yourself and the world as a whole. Use art and words to convey the suffering, being as personal or as universal as you want. This will be your wrapping paper.

~ Buy for yourself a Christmas present, or choose something you already value.

~ Using the paper, carefully wrap the present in the 'suffering' paper. Feel free to add ribbons and decoration, valuing it as you would any other present. There is beauty and grace even in the suffering.

~ During a quiet moment at Christmas, unwrap the gift slowly, and meditate on this verse: "I consider that our present sufferings are not worth comparing with the glory that will be revealed in us" (Romans 8:18).

We have travelled with:

~ **Sarah** - who wrestled with disappointment and bitterness as she waited to be included in God's plan for a family to bless the world.

~ **Isaiah** - who wrestled with frustration and impatience as he anticipated God's coming judgment of injustice and salvation of those who longed for peace.

~ **John the Baptist** - who wrestled with waiting for his calling, then wrestled with doubt and despair as he waited alone for freedom or death.

~ **Mary, Mother of Jesus** - who dealt with isolation and disgrace as she waited for the best thing in history - the coming of Christ.

And through it all we have seen God, who:

~ Saw **Sarah** when others didn't, honoured Sarah where her husband hadn't, and granted her heart's desire, even though she was bitter and disbelieving.

~ Gave **Isaiah** a vision of God's divine nature that would sustain him through his difficult ministry.

~ Loves justice and cares for the vulnerable.

~ Gave reassurance to **John** when he needed it most and celebrated him and his ministry.

~ Loved **Mary**, provided Joseph for her and honoured her faith.

We have wrestled with the mystery of God's delay but have seen glimpses of grace and mercy along the way.

~ **Sarah's** story reminds us that the joy to come is even greater than the pain of now.

~ **Isaiah's** story reminds us that sometimes the waiting is a mercy - often God delays the negative consequences of our actions so we have a chance to change our behaviour and respond.

~ **John the Baptist's** story tells us that sometimes we spend our whole lives waiting - and then waiting again - and yet we are honoured and loved in the sight of God.

~ **Mary's** story reminds us of the true focus of our lives, whatever else we are waiting for: Jesus.

Remembering Promises

In my retellings of Sarah, Mary, and John, I have emphasised how words from God sustained them during hard times as they reflected on God's character or God's actions in the past. One thing that helps in hanging onto the promises of God is the discipline of remembering and reflecting. If you have a journal, flick back through it; if you have chosen a verse, word, or resolution for this year, consider how God has been in the midst of it.

Take a look back through the year and consider:

~ What are the ways that God has been faithful to you and good to you this year?

~ What are some of the promises that God has spoken to you particularly this year? Pause and write them down. (Even if you're not sure if they're from God, write them down anyway.)

~ What are some of the promises from the Bible that have been particularly important for you this year? Write them down.

~ How have you heard God's voice this year? In a whisper? A shout? In the silence? Journal or doodle these thoughts and reflections.

Some of these reflections and exercises are repeated in the Group Bible Study.

This is the end of the main book, but for those who are interested in how much of the story is based in the Bible or tradition rather than my imagination, there follows a Question and Answer section on the historical context and theological choices I made.

Additionally, there are six Bible studies for group study that can accompany the book or stand alone - plus Author's Acknowledgements and details of how you can keep in touch.

APPENDIX A
Theological Choices and Historical Notes

Notes for Sarah's Story

When and where did Abraham and Sarah live?

Four thousand years ago, in the Middle Bronze Age, approximately 1900 BC, Abraham and Sarah lived in the Mesopotamian region. Mesopotamia means 'between two rivers', because it was between the Tigris and Euphrates rivers. At that time, In the Ancient Near East in Abraham and Sarah's time, they practised intensive agriculture, they had formalised worship, and they established a rule of law within a stratified and hierarchical society. The invention of the fast potter's wheel made pottery much more common. Some cultures had even developed the earliest form of writing: in Egypt, hieroglyphs; in Mesopotamia, cuneiform writing.

Would the pyramids have been built in Egypt by then?

There were various pyramids built at different times. In Giza, the three important pyramids were built c. 2600-2500 BC, which was 600-700 years before Abraham and Sarah's time. It's fascinating to think that, by the time Abraham and Sarah saw Pharaoh, the pyramids would already be revered as historical sites.

Where is Ur?

It is thought to have been in modern-day Iraq, about ten miles southwest of Nasiriyah. It was a centre of civilisation; a metropolis with a rich cultural, religious and historical heritage.

What was the local religion?

Mesopotamian religion was based around the concept of warring deities, who were to be feared and appeased, but not known personally. People offered up sacrifices to these many and various gods - sometimes human sacrifices - and would visit temple prostitutes, who were associated with the worship of a fertility god. Each city adopted a particular deity to worship. For Ur, that god was Nanna, the moon god. Temple worship for

Nanna would have been a major feature of Ur. Historian Tertius Chandler estimated the population to be 65,000. We assume that Abraham grew up here, as his father and family started off in Ur.

What was Harran like?

Harran, sometimes called Haran, was a place 600 miles northwest of Ur, towards Canaan. Harran was still within Mesopotamia, which today would cover an area in Iraq and Iran. Harran was much smaller than Canaan, with a population of 20,000. It functioned as a crossroads for people travelling the east/west trade routes between Mesopotamia and the Mediterranean.

Harran was also associated with the worship of Nanna, which may have been a motivator for Terah remaining in Harran rather than going on to Canaan, though we are never told this.

What was special about Mamre?

Mamre is the place in which Abraham and Sarah had settled when the visitors came to them. It was in Canaan, in a plain, at, or very near, ancient Hebron, about twenty miles south of Jerusalem. It was known for its large oak, 'terebinth', trees and associated with idol worship.

See http://cookingwiththebible.com/reader/print.aspx?id=GR3410-132&type=recipe (accessed May 2017) for a suggestion and recipe of what Abraham and Sarah might have cooked for the messengers. It looks tasty.

Was Terah, Abraham's father, alive when Abraham left Harran?

I am indebted to Charlotte Gordon for highlighting the chronology:
* Genesis 11:26 says Abraham was born when Terah was seventy.
* Genesis 11:32 tells us that Terah died in Harran when he was 205 years old.

The biblical narrative then jumps to Abraham's call and journey in Genesis 12, giving the impression that his call came after his father's death. However, Genesis 12:4 tells us that Abraham left Harran when he was aged 75, which would have placed Terah at age 145. This would have given Terah another sixty years alive.

This makes Abraham's leaving all the more surprising - that in a patriarchal society he should come out from his father's authority and abandon him. It is the most counter-cultural call you could imagine. Because he left his father, Abraham would probably have been seen as a rebel; a heartless, faithless son; an utter disgrace.

Joshua 24:2 tells us that Terah worshipped other (pagan) gods. This is possibly why God called Abraham away from that household and lifestyle. As far as we know, Abraham never reconciles with or returns to his father.

Haran, Abraham's middle brother, dies while Terah is alive, but probably the remaining brother, Nahor, stayed in Harran (the place) with Terah. In Genesis 22 we discover Nahor has had children, and in Genesis 24:24 Rebecca is named as Nahor's (Abraham's brother's) granddaughter, living in Nahor (the place), which is either Harran or very near it, in Upper Mesopotamia. (To add to the confusion, Terah's father, Abraham's grandfather, is also named Nahor.)

Was Sarah really Abraham's half-sister?

Because Abraham later specifically tells Abimelek this in Genesis 20:12, claiming it to be truth - and it is not contradicted in the text - it is a possibility that they were indeed half-siblings. However, many commentators have questioned why, if this were the case, that Sarah wasn't mentioned as Terah's daughter in the thorough family tree in Genesis 11. In Jewish tradition, the Talmud (Sanhedrin 69B) has identified her as being one and the same as Iscah, daughter of Haran, which would make her Abraham's niece rather than sister. There may be the linguistic flexibility for 'sister' to be translated more like 'kinswoman'. For example, Lot is described as Abraham's 'brother' in Genesis 14:16, although in Genesis 11 he's listed as Haran's son, Abraham's nephew. Other commentators theorise that it was a complete fabrication on Abraham's part, showing him to be a liar but not guilty of incest.

So the possibilities are:
1) Even when Abraham claims to be telling the truth, he is still lying to Abimelek and Sarah is not his relative at all (which is why she's not mentioned in the Genesis 11 family tree)
2) Sarah is Abraham's half-sister. She's not mentioned as Terah's daughter only because it's more important that she was Abraham's wife
3) Sarah is Abraham's close relative or niece, though not sister.

The interpretation I find most convincing is the first option: that Abraham was lying. However, in my telling I've evaded the question nicely by calling them 'family' and describing them growing up together: they could have been half-siblings, other relatives, or close childhood friends, growing up in the same village.

Just supposing Abraham and Sarah were half-siblings, would they not have been sinning by having an incestuous marriage?

Though abhorrent to us now, it is worth noting that the Levitical law prohibiting incestuous marriage did not come in for another 400 years.

What's the theological significance of Sarah's Egyptian experience?

Interestingly, Sarah's experience foreshadows Israel's future slavery in Egypt. She is in bondage to Pharaoh until God afflicts Pharaoh's household with illnesses (like the plagues).

Did Abraham repent of prostituting his wife to a powerful ruler?

Sadly, it seems not. Abraham doesn't learn from the experience: he does the same thing again to Sarah in Genesis 20:1-18, when he visits Abimelek. Once again, God intervenes, this time with a supernatural dream, and Abimelek sends them both away unharmed.

Did Pharaoh sleep with Sarah?

Does Pharaoh's statement, "I took her for my wife," mean that she was merely added to his harem, or that he 'took' her body and consummated the marriage? In Genesis 20:6 it also says that Abimelek 'took' Sarah, but later clarifies that the Lord did not let Abimelek 'touch' Sarah. There are therefore two ways of reading it: the first, that the detail in the Abimelek story helps to interpret and clarify the Pharaoh story; the second, that the Abimelek story contrasts with the Pharaoh story.

I understand the two stories as a pattern of similarity, assuming that if God had protected her with Abimelek, God would have protected Sarah in Egypt, too. However, there are those who have come to the opposite conclusion - that because it does not explicitly say in Genesis 12 that Pharaoh did not touch Sarah, he most likely slept with her. The text gives room for both interpretations, so I have consciously left the story a little ambiguous. In my retelling, we're not told what happens in the night to Sarah, and when she awakes, aching and sore, it could be from the pain of rape, or just the pain of the journey. I've left it for the reader to interpret.

Did Hagar know Abraham and Sarah from Egypt?

We know two things: Abraham and Sarah left Egypt with wealth, including male and female servants (Genesis 12:16, 20), and that Hagar was an Egyptian slave. It is possible that she was one of Pharaoh's 'gifts' from Egypt. Some ancient writers believed her to be an Egyptian princess (which could explain why Hagar was singled out to be the surrogate), but that goes beyond the Bible text. Though I didn't explore it in the text, it's interesting to consider what their relationship could have been like: friends, perhaps; or maybe Hagar reminded Sarah of dark times in Egypt.

What was the difference between Abraham and Sarah's old names versus the new ones?

I'm indebted to Paula Gooder for pointing out that the change in meaning is there for Abraham and Sarah, but barely. Both Sarai and Sarah mean 'princess'. However, whereas Sarai could be translated 'my princess', belonging to someone, Sarah couldn't be translated that way: she is honoured in her own right. Abram's name was changed from 'father' to 'father of many nations', giving Abraham a vision of the future. In both their names there is an extra syllable, like a breath, which some say is associated either with the name of God or the breath of God.

What happened to Sarah after Isaac?

The end of my retelling is not the end of Sarah's story. It would be nice to look upon her as a hero who was completely rid of her bitterness after Isaac's birth, but she was a real and flawed person, and the Bible doesn't try to conceal that in the name of making a happy ending. Sadly, having waited for so long for Isaac, she becomes insecure and possessive of her son, not able to relax or trust God that Isaac's future would be safe. Despite having given birth to the heir, she still feels threatened by Hagar and Ishmael. The last words we hear from her are chilling, casting out Hagar and her son into the desert (where they could have died).

Though I would not want to excuse her actions, I think taking a deeper look at Sarah's story helps us understand them. Abraham's habit of 'pimping out' his wife to dignitaries - not just with Pharaoh, but also Abimelek - sets up a pattern of abuse, and Sarah in turn abuses her power over her subordinates. I would argue, as Jenni Williams does in *God*

Remembered Rachel,[16] that although Sarah became a bully, she was, in part, 'made monstrous' by the previous events of her life.

Whereas Abraham has further interactions with the Lord, Sarah is deprived of such conversations, so we never know quite what became of her faith and walk with God. In the Bible, Sarah is an ambiguous character, possibly because she is not given a voice in the way that Abraham is. We never hear whether she ultimately ended her life in repentant faith or hardened bitterness. However, she lived a long life, often seen in those times as a reward from God for faithfulness. She was buried in what became the family tomb, near the spot where the angels of the Lord visited them, in Mamre, Canaan - the land they had travelled so long to reach. In the New Testament she is praised as a good and obedient wife to Abraham (1 Peter 3:6), but also as a woman of faith, who believed God's promise. She was honoured in the 'cloud of witnesses' list of Hebrews 11 as a woman of faith who, like us, was a broken, ordinary, beloved saint, called to follow God into the unknown.

---

[16] Jenni Williams, *God Remembered Rachel*, SPCK, 2013

Notes for Isaiah's Story

Names of rulers and countries

At the time of Isaiah's confrontation with King Ahaz in Isaiah 7:
- ~ **Ahaz** was the king of **Judah,** the Southern Kingdom, which had **Jerusalem** as its capital.
- ~ **Pekah** was the king of **Israel/ Ephraim**, the Northern Kingdom, sometimes referred to by its capital, **Samaria.**
- ~ **Rezin** was the King of **Aram/ Syria**, sometimes referred to by its capital, **Damascus.**
- ~ **Tiglath-Pileser III** led **Assyria**, the up-and-coming superpower. Its capital was **Kalhu,** known in the Bible as Calah or **Nimrud.**

Under the rule of David's son, King Solomon, Israel was a united kingdom, consisting of the twelve tribes of Israel. However, after Solomon, the Kingdom of Israel split in two: 'Judah' in the South, and 'Israel' in the North.

Despite the fact that the Northern Kingdom kept the name and ten out of the twelve tribes, Judah was viewed as the 'true' kingdom. This was because Judah's kings descended from Solomon, God's temple was in its capital, Jerusalem, and Israel's rulers tended to be more sinful than Judah's.

Where in the Bible does it mention people being driven out of Elath?

2 Kings 16:6.

What were some of the injustices in Judah at the time?

Isaiah 1-5 describes the backdrop of the sins of Israel when Isaiah was ministering. God says Judah is like a vineyard, cared for by God but yielding only bad fruit (Isaiah 5). Read Isaiah 3:16-4:1 for specific details of the women who were dressed in finery but ignored the cries of the poor. God would not let this behaviour go unchecked.

Timeline for reference

This is my (very rough) timeline. All of these dates are up for negotiation, and are approximate. In the main, I've followed Oswald's analysis.[17] He argues that the oracles in Isaiah 1-11 are arranged thematically, so the chronology jumps, sometimes by decades, between each section. The kings referred to are the kings of Judah, where Isaiah was based.

740 BC   **King Uzziah dies.** Also known as Azariah, he had been reigning for fifty-two years (see 2 Kings 15:1-7). King Jotham accedes to the throne.

740 BC   In the year King Uzziah dies, **Isaiah's vision in temple** (see Isaiah 6). **Shear-Jashub** born this year.

734 BC   **King Ahaz** comes to the throne. (Maybe 732 BC)

732 BC   **Isaiah confronts King Ahaz** at the aqueduct of the Upper Pool, and tells him not to worry about Aram and Israel. **Shear-Jashub** is c. 8 years old. (See Isaiah 7:1-25 and 2 Kings 16:1-20 on the outcome: King Ahaz was besieged by Aram and Israel, and subsequently Ahaz signs an alliance with Assyria.)

732 BC   **Damascus** (capital of Syria/Aram) **falls to Assyria.** This is most likely the fulfilment of Isaiah's promise to King Ahaz that Judah need not fear Syria because Syria's defeat would be swift. Israel's defeat takes a little longer.

731 BC   **Birth of Maher-Shalal-Hash-Baz,** Isaiah's second son (see Isaiah 8).

729 BC   **King Hezekiah,** a more godly king than Ahaz, rules with Ahaz as co-regent.

722 BC   **Samaria** (capital of Israel/Ephraim) **is besieged by Assyrians,** and they are exiled.

716 BC   **King Hezekiah** is sole king (and rules till c. 680 BC).

710 BC   **Isaiah has a vision of future hope,** from the stump of Jesse, Isaiah 11 (Isaiah is aged c. 70, Shear-Jashub c. 30-37, Baz c. 22).

701 BC   **Isaiah dies.**

---

[17] John N Oswalt, *The Book of Isaiah, Chapters 1-39,* NICOT, Eerdmans, 1996

What do we definitely know about Isaiah's family from the Bible?

The short answer is not much. His father was named Amoz (not to be confused with the prophet Amos); Isaiah had a wife; he had at least two children, Shear-Jashub and Maher-Shalal-Hash-Baz. See below for explanations about why I made the choices I did.

What do we know about Isaiah's father?

Isaiah is frequently referred to as 'Isaiah, son of Amoz'. The Talmudic understanding was that if a prophet's father was named in the text, it's because their father was a prophet himself (see Talmud tractate Megillah 15a), which is a supposition I explored in my story.

Was Isaiah of royal blood?

Additionally, there is a (disputed) tradition that Amoz, Isaiah's father, was the brother of King Amaziah, and was the 'man of God' who rebuked Amaziah in 2 Chronicles 25:7. This would make Isaiah of royal blood. I haven't pressed this possible connection to royalty.

However, there is good reason for believing that Isaiah was at least from the ruling classes: he writes as someone well-educated, he had good access to the royal courts in Jerusalem, and his bold confrontations were tolerated well by the kings of Judah. I like the idea that he functioned as a 'royal chaplain', and was a thorn in the side of the kings, whom they had to tolerate.

Manasseh, son of Hezekiah, is possibly the exception. Tradition has it that Isaiah died by being sawn in half at Manasseh's command (there is possible support for that in Hebrews 11:37, though it doesn't specifically mention Isaiah). However, this would not match the approximate timeline I'm working with.

How many 'sign-children' are there?

There are four mentions of sign-children, though not necessarily four separate children - some descriptions may overlap.

~ **Shear-Jashub** (meaning 'a remnant will return') was possibly a sign to King Ahaz, which is why Isaiah brought him along to the meeting at the aqueduct (Isaiah 7:3).

~ **Immanuel** is the second, and most famous sign-child (Isaiah 7:14-16). It is not known for sure who the child was in Isaiah's understanding (see further discussion below), but Matthew applies it prophetically to Jesus (Matthew 1:23) as support for Mary's virgin birth.

~ **Maher-Shalal-Hash-Baz** - Isaiah's child, born to the prophetess or 'wife of the prophet' (Isaiah 8:1-4).

~ **"Unto us a child is born"** (Isaiah 9:6-7) - the descriptions of this child apply to a future Messiah, understood by Christians to be Jesus.

The Problem of Immanuel

"Therefore the Lord himself will give you a sign: The virgin [*better translation: maiden*] will conceive and give birth to a son, and will call him Immanuel. He will be eating curds and honey when he knows enough to reject the wrong and choose the right, for before the boy knows enough to reject the wrong and choose the right, the land of the two kings you dread will be laid waste. The Lord will bring on you and on your people and on the house of your father a time unlike any since Ephraim broke away from Judah - he will bring the king of Assyria." - Isaiah 7:14-17, NIV UK.

But I thought the prophecies were solely specific to Jesus?

Prophetic fulfilment doesn't have to be either Jesus, or someone in Isaiah's day. It doesn't have to be an 'either/or', it can be a 'both/and'.

If you have never seen Old Testament prophecy working in this way before (the initial fulfilment was in the prophet's day, but later writers applied the prophecy to Jesus) then it may feel uncomfortable. Does this make the Bible any less powerful or reliable if the prophecies of Jesus also apply to events in Isaiah's time? Don't they have to apply uniquely to Jesus in order to be true prophecy?

To answer this, we need to have an understanding of the Old Testament view of history. We in the twenty-first century West tend to view history as linear: x happened, which led to y, which led to z. In ancient times, they thought of history as cyclical, with patterns repeating over the years: x1, y1, z1 happened, and then x2, y2, z2, and we can expect x3, y3, z3 in the future. This is subtly different to an Eastern understanding of reincarnation, which repeats cycles without a sense of moving towards progress: XYZ, over and over. The Bible's picture of time is both cyclical *and* forward-moving, with each new revolution bringing fresh insight.

Gooder envisages this view of history as a snowball rolling down a hill, gathering more snow each time it rolls, adding more layers to the sphere.[18] Ecclesiastes 1:9 explains this philosophy: "What has been will be again, what has been done will be done again; there is nothing new under the sun." In *Journey to the Manger*,[19] Gooder explains that for ancient readers, rather than make a prophecy less accurate or powerful, finding precedent in a previous event *enhanced* its reliability as a historical source:

"In our context, something copied or borrowed from the past might be considered less true rather than more true; in the ancient world the opposite was the case. If you could prove that the story you told was old or that the roots of your beliefs went far back into history, this would demonstrate that what you said was reliable and trustworthy." (*Journey to the Manger*, p. xi)

Does the child 'Immanuel' refer to Jesus, or a child born in Isaiah's time?

Probably both. In Isaiah 7, we are told that a maiden, i.e. someone who was at that point unmarried and therefore, in that culture, likely also a virgin, would conceive (presumably in the normal way). Before the child was either 3 or 12, depending on your definition of 'knowing right from wrong', destruction would come on Aram and Ephraim. That child would be called 'Immanuel', meaning 'God with us'.

The prophecy is specific to Isaiah's time and place. The point is that the destruction of these countries is imminent so God's people will be saved. (However, Ahaz doesn't listen to Isaiah, so Judah is later plundered by Assyria as judgement.) The reference to 'virgin' in Isaiah's time didn't necessarily signify a miraculous virgin birth, but simply that the woman was at that point unmarried. Isaiah uses the Hebrew word *almah*, meaning a maiden, of marriageable age but not married, as opposed to the usual Hebrew word specifically for virgin, *bethulah*. Matthew translates *almah* as the Greek word *parthenos*, which carries the narrower meaning of 'virgin'.

In Isaiah's time, the prophecy meant that a virgin conceived in the ordinary way and called her son Immanuel. However, Matthew takes that verse and applies it prophetically to Jesus as the ultimate sign-child for Judah. As the divine Messiah, Jesus was Immanuel, literally God-with-us. Matthew sees in Isaiah 7 not merely a prediction of an unmarried woman becoming pregnant, but a virgin supernaturally impregnated by the Holy Spirit: Mary therefore remained a virgin at the time of giving *birth*, not just

---

[18] Paula Gooder, *The Meaning is the Waiting: The Spirit of Advent,* Canterbury Press, 2008, pp8-10

[19] Paula Gooder, Journey to the Manger, (Canterbury Press, 2015)

at Jesus' *conception*. The partial fulfilment in Isaiah paved the way for a greater sign-child later.

Paula Gooder explains it in this way:

"This [Isaiah 7:14-17] is a prophecy about God's imminent salvation of the people of God. The message is clear; once this child is born you should be on the lookout for salvation as it will only be a matter of time before it breaks on the world. Matthew seems to be using this as a pledge for the future: once you see this event [Jesus' birth] taking place you will know that salvation is near." (Paula Gooder, *The Meaning is in the Waiting*, p.44)

The original readers of Matthew's gospel would have been very familiar with the events of Isaiah, but less familiar with the miracle of Jesus' birth. For those of us steeped in a church upbringing, we are likely to be very familiar with Jesus' nativity story, but less familiar with the context of Isaiah's words. My hope is that as we explore what the situation was like for Isaiah, we shall see that there is 'nothing new under the sun', and from the roots of story that emerge from Isaiah we can see shoots into Jesus' story, and indeed our own.

Aside from Jesus, who else does the Immanuel prophecy refer to (in Isaiah's time)?

The short answer? No one really knows. "Unfortunately, almost every word of the sign given in vv. 14ff. is controversial," admits Brevard S Childs.[20] This is my quick guided tour through the main options for a 'first Immanuel child':

1) There was no Immanuel child born in Isaiah's day; it just applied to Jesus.[21]

2) Hezekiah (King Ahaz's son) or another royal child is Immanuel.[22]

---

[20] From Brevard S Childs, *Isaiah*, Westminster John Knox Press, 2001, p. 65

[21] Some say it was a failed prophecy, because its fulfilment is not recorded in Isaiah's book. But it would be stranger to record a false prophecy by such a revered prophet. How could Isaiah insist on it as a sign if Ahaz didn't witness it?

[22] Chapter 8 says the land 'belongs' to Immanuel. This suggests King Ahaz's eldest song, Hezekiah, who would inherit the land. However, most scholars agree that Hezekiah was six years old when the prophecy was given, so it doesn't make sense for this to be a prediction of his birth.

3) A generation of children from Judah named Immanuel, as a sign to Ahaz.[23]

4) A child born to an ordinary maiden in Judah.[24]

Or, my favoured explanation:

5) Immanuel is a child born to Isaiah, probably Maher-Shalal-Hash-Baz.

Hezekiah or Maher-Shalal-Hash-Baz?

All five options have support from various Christian scholars. The most popular explanations for the identity of the 'first Immanuel child', both in rabbinic thought and Christian theology, are evenly split between Hezekiah (King Ahaz's son) and Maher-Shalal-Hash-Baz (Isaiah's second son). Isaiah 7 prophesies a sign-child, Immanuel, who would herald the imminent destruction of Aram and Ephraim. In the very next chapter, God tells Isaiah he will have a child 'Baz', who would be a *sign* that Aram and Ephraim would soon be destroyed.

This is too much of a coincidence for theologians to ignore. Though Isaiah's child isn't named Immanuel, the timing of Baz's birth makes this a strong case.

I was persuaded that Isaiah 7 is (partially) fulfilled in Isaiah's second son Maher-Shalal-Hash-Baz, following both John N. Oswalt and Herbert M. Wolf's[25] interpretations of Isaiah 7-8.

However, this interpretation gave me a creative and theological problem:

---

[23] 'Maiden' could possibly be taken as a group of women, but Childs maintains that there's a particular sign-child in the prophecy, rather than many children.

[24] There could have been a maiden, perhaps a servant or cousin there, known to both Isaiah and Ahaz, engaged to be married, to whom Isaiah was referring. This is possible, but conjecture.

[25] See Oswalt, pp 202-214, and Herbert Martin Wolf, "Solution to the Immanuel prophecy in Isaiah 7:14-8:22," Journal of Biblical Literature 91.4 (Dec. 1972): 449-456. Wolf argues that the 'witnesses' were there not only to witness the prophecy, but also the marriage ceremony. He understands M-S-H-B's conception as the first sexual union between Isaiah and his new wife.

If the first Immanuel sign-child was born to an unmarried woman, and Isaiah had already had a son, how could M-S-H-Baz be the same as the promised Immanuel sign-child?

Isaiah 7 tells us that Isaiah already has a son, Shear-Jashub.

In Isaiah 8, which, by my timeline, took place almost a decade later, Isaiah conceives another son with a woman known as 'the prophetess' (which might have meant she was a prophet in her own right, or that she was already the wife of the prophet). For the purpose of my story, I named her Nevi'a, which, when translated, is 'prophetess' or 'wife of the prophet'. I saw it as a classic case of nominative determinism.

Was 'the prophetess' of Isaiah 8 already Isaiah's wife and the mother of Shear-Jashub? In that case, she couldn't be a 'maiden/virgin' prophesied in Isaiah 7.

If we suppose 'the prophetess' was a maiden, and therefore not the mother of Shear-Jashub, was Isaiah polygamous? These questions go unanswered in the Bible, so they're all possibilities.

To neaten things up, Wolf suggests that Isaiah's first wife, mother of Shear-Jeshub, had died, perhaps after childbirth. Isaiah, the widower, then married the prophetess. This hypothesis would make the new wife, Nevi'a, a 'maiden' at the point of conception, and would hint at their child being the prophesied Immanuel, whilst not proving it definitely (cf Oswalt, p. 222). For this hypothesis to work, Isaiah would have to marry her immediately after the prophecy, with their marriage consummation as Baz's conception (Isaiah 8).

Although there is no mention in the Bible of a first wife, this would explain the long gap between the birth of Shear-Jashub, and Baz, with no children mentioned in-between.

All of the possibilities of the immediate identity of Immanuel have their problems. None fit neatly into the Bible text, which is why more ink has been spilt on these chapters than almost any other in the Bible! In my retelling, I wanted to leave all the possibilities open as far as possible for the reader to explore, which made it necessary to be vague about Hezekiah's age (in case he was the sign-child). In the main, though, I follow Wolf's interpretation.

While we can only guess the identity of the Immanuel-child in Isaiah's day, we do know Isaiah was right about the imminent defeat of Aram and Ephraim.

However, this prophecy also looks beyond Isaiah's immediate situation and finds its fulfilment in Christ. Isaiah prophesied a child, born of a maiden, who would be 'God-with-us'. When Jesus came, his followers recognised Jesus as the Immanuel promised all those years before: the ultimate God-with-us sign-child who would bring true peace.

Why is it bad that Ahaz doesn't want to ask for a sign?

In Isaiah 7, Isaiah invites King Ahaz to ask God for a sign that the two countries he was fearing would soon fall. But Ahaz refuses. When he refuses, Isaiah grows angry - but why? Surely it's bad to 'put God to the test'?[26] The most plausible explanation for Isaiah's anger is because he sees the reason behind Ahaz's refusal: Ahaz has already decided to sign an alliance with Assyria. Essentially, Ahaz is rejecting the word of God, though in the politest possible terms.

What's the significance of the curds and honey? (Isaiah 7:22)

In some contexts in the Bible, curds and honey is a sign of abundance, blessing or even a royal food. But the more likely explanation in this context is that it's a sign of desolation and curse: food of the desert, living off whatever you could find (goat curds and honey). This is supported by the description of the landscape in Isaiah 7:23-25, where the previously fertile land is now covered in briars and thorns.

However, it could be a sign of God's providence in a desert place: although judgement will be swift, there would still be some indications of *Immanuel* - God with them in the midst of destruction. Likewise, the sign child would have this double-meaning: "For those of unbelief - Ahaz and his people - the sign is one of destruction (v.17), but for those of belief, the sign of Immanuel is a pledge of God's continuing presence in salvation (v.16)" (Childs, p. 68).

When was the prophecy of Isaiah 11 written?

Isaiah is arranged 'logically, not chronologically' (Oswalt), so between chapters 7 and 11 there could be some twenty years. Oswalt estimates the prophecies of Isaiah 10 and 11 to have been delivered sometime between 717 and 701 BC, because the defeat of Carchemish by Assyria (mentioned in Is 10:8) didn't occur till 717 BC (Oswalt, p. 262). I'm not sure how Isaiah received his prophecies from God, so I have imagined what it might have looked like for him, based on others' contemporary experiences of hearing prophecy from God.

---

[26] See Deut 6:16, Luke 4:12, Matt 4:7

Was Isaiah a grandfather when he gave the prophecy of Isaiah 11?

Quite possibly. I've loosely placed the prophecy of Isaiah 11 in 710 BC, which is in the middle of the 16-year window that Oswalt and others estimate. Assuming Shear-Jashub was between eight and fifteen years old when he went up with Isaiah to confront King Ahaz, this would have made him between 30-37 years old in 710 BC, and Baz approximately 22. A Jewish male could be married as a young teen, so both sons would easily be old enough to be married, with children.

Notes for John's Story

Why does John the Baptist keep leaping at Jesus?

Luke 1 tells us John the Baptist leapt in his mother's womb when Mary came to visit. I thought it would be fun to continue the theme. Elizabeth, John's mother, recognises that Mary's baby is even more important than her own: "But why am I so favoured, that the mother of my Lord should come to me?" (Luke 1:43) This is how she 'had her own ideas' about who the Messiah would be.

Was John related to Jesus?

Yes. Luke tells us that Mary visited her 'relative' Elizabeth - the word could mean cousins or a more distant relative. Since John the Baptist appears not to have met Jesus before he baptises him, one can assume that either they were too distantly related to meet at family reunions, or perhaps they lost touch when the families fled to escape Herod's slaughtering of young boys.

What was prophesied about John the Baptist when he was a baby?

When in the temple, Zechariah met the angel Gabriel, who prophesied that he and his wife, who had struggled with infertility, would have a son. Their son was to be dedicated to the Lord and not drink alcohol. He would be filled with the Spirit, even in the womb; he would be a prophet to the people of Israel, and his commission was this:

"And he will go on before the Lord, **in the spirit and power of Elijah**, to turn the hearts of the parents to their children and the disobedient to the wisdom of the righteous – **to make ready a people prepared for the Lord.**" (Luke 1:17).

When John is born, Zechariah sings a joyful song which indicates the kind of person his community expected John to be: one who would bring 'salvation from our enemies and from the hand of all who hate us' (Luke 1:71) and who would 'rescue us from the hand of our enemies, and to enable us to serve [God] without fear.' (Luke 1:74) You can see how this prophetic song would raise expectations that the Roman overlords would be defeated, so God's people could serve the Lord in full peace and freedom.

For how long was John in the wilderness, and why?

Luke 1:80 tells us that John 'grew and became strong in spirit; and he lived in the wilderness until he appeared publicly to Israel'. Some have taken this to mean that John spent his childhood in the wilderness, possibly with an ascetic community such as the Essenes of the Qumran sect. Some have suggested that he went to the wilderness to escape from Herod the Great's clutches.

Normally, around 12 or 13 was the minimum age a Jewish child would be considered an adult, but a priest would not have been allowed on the temple 'rota' till he was 30 or so. That leaves a gap of at least ten years. Normally, during this time, a priest would have been rooted in a local community while studying and teaching the Torah (the first five books of the Bible) and associated teaching. I have assumed that he went into the wilderness for this time. Rather than being taught by a spiritual community, I have imagined that God taught him through creation itself.

Which Herod did John criticise?

Herod the Great was the 'King Herod' of the time of Jesus' birth. Herod the Great had his doubts about which son should succeed him as king, so in his final will he divided up the title and land, leaving the bulk of it to Archelaus (who became ethnarch, rather than King, and ruled Judea and Samaria). Antipas and his brother Philip were 'tetrarchs' (i.e. governors who ruled over a quarter of a province): Antipas governed Galilee and Perea; Philip governed the Golan Heights and northern territories. Antipas and Philip ruled over neighbouring areas. You can see how it might be politically unwise to marry your brother's wife, especially when she was the daughter of your other half-brother Aristobulus - and you were already married. This was incest and adultery, wildly breaking the law of Moses. John the Baptist condemned the marriage as immoral.

Although Mark 6:14 refers to him as 'King' Herod, Herod Antipas was more properly a governor, with decidedly less power than his father. Antipas would be succeeded by Agrippa, whom Paul would face later.

Where was John imprisoned?

According to Josephus, the place where Herod Antipas imprisoned and beheaded John was Fortress Machaerus, situated on a high hill in the middle of the Judean desert, 15km south of Jerusalem. The prison and the palace were part of the same building, and it would have been very busy and noisy. It may be fanciful, but possible, that John the Baptist would therefore have heard the music coming from the palace party while he was in prison.

He was probably chained, and may have been in solitary confinement, or with other prisoners. In some prisons of that time, both prisoners and visitors were let down through a hole to the cell at the bottom, with a rope for the visitors to climb up again. The fortress may have operated in this way, or it may have been guarded with cells along corridors, as we tend to imagine ancient prisons. Food may have been carried to John this way, and also straw (to help clear the mess associated with the lack of an ensuite bathroom in his prison cell). In any case, it would have been dark, lonely and smelly.

The prison would have provided meagre rations, if anything at all. John would have been dependent on his friends to keep him fed.

For how long was John imprisoned?

Probably just under two years. The timings are estimated from the mention of Passovers in Jesus' ministry. At the first Passover in Jesus ministry, John's gospel tells us that John the Baptist was not yet in prison (John 3:24). The synoptic gospels (Matthew, Mark, Luke) mention John the Baptist's death just before the feeding of the five thousand, and in John's gospel the feeding of the thousand coincides roughly with the third Passover of Jesus' ministry, about a year before Jesus' death. This gives us an approximate timeline.

Was imprisonment usual as a punishment?

John the Baptist's imprisonment was an unusually long one. Prisons were not generally used as punishments for a crime as we see them today: they were a place you stayed temporarily while your fate was decided. Normally, prisons acted as 'holding cells' for those who had been arrested and were awaiting trial, or those who'd been sentenced, awaiting execution. Wealthier prisoners were often kept on house arrest and then taken to trial (like Paul); poorer prisoners were much more likely to have met their death sooner rather than later. Mark's gospel tells us that Herod couldn't quite make up his mind which of these outcomes he wanted for John the Baptist, which is why he held him for so long.

Why did Herod behead John?

According to Mark 6, Herod's new wife Herodias hated John for condemning their marriage. Herodias' daughter danced for Herod Antipas and charmed him so that he made a rash promise to give her whatever she requested. She asked for John the Baptist's head. Antipas, not wanting to renege on his promise in front of all his dinner guests, had John beheaded then and there.

Jesus as a new Joshua?

We call him Jesus, but his friends probably would have called him Yeshua, a version of Joshua. I enjoyed playing with the idea of John as a new Moses, bringing people back to repentance and the holy law of God, with Jesus as the new Joshua who figuratively leads people into the Promised Land.

Notes for Mary's Story

Did the angel bow to Mary?

We're not told the angel's posture, nor of any pauses. However, inspired by Da Vinci's Annunciation painting, I liked the idea of Gabriel bowing to Mary, indicating her importance.

How old would Mary have been when she gave birth to Jesus?

Although some have estimated Mary to have been between fifteen and twenty when she married, Paula Gooder explains that the normal age for marriage in Roman law was twelve for girls and fourteen for boys. Jewish law was similar, so that the virginity of the girl was ensured. It was possible for girls to be betrothed at the age of eleven. In the story, I have assumed a little later, around fourteen for betrothal and fifteen for marriage. I have tried to reflect her age in her voice.

Would Mary have been stoned for adultery?

Betrothal was closer to our idea of marriage than our modern term of 'engagement'. The contract would be drawn up, money handed over, and they would be referred to as 'husband' and 'wife' though the couple would not have sexual intercourse until after the wedding. You would need a divorce to break a betrothal. The girl would live at her father's house for a year, then she would move to the groom's house when she was old enough for marriage. After betrothal, you would be understood to be husband and wife, even though the marriage was not yet consummated.

Although the law of Moses stipulates that adultery is punishable by death by stoning (Deuteronomy 22:23-25), this seems to have been practised very infrequently. More common was divorce, which Matthew tells us is what Joseph planned to do. After the angel came to Joseph, however, he took Mary to be his wife (i.e. they married and she lived in his house), though the text emphasises that they did not sleep together before the baby was born.

Did Mary waver in her faith?

Some may interpret my retelling of Mary's nightmare and questions about seeing an angel as a sinful kind of doubt. I view Mary as a person full of faith, and note that Elizabeth particularly praised Mary for believing in God's promises. However, within the realm of belief and faith, I think there is room for a little fear and questions without it being necessarily sinful.

Why is Joseph listed as Jesus' father in the genealogies of the gospels when he wasn't the biological father?

This is because he adopted Jesus as his own, and all the rights of inheritance were transferred to Jesus. (Joseph was a good'un.)

Was Joseph much older than Mary?

There is good evidence in the Bible text to assume that Joseph died early; sometime after Jesus was twelve years old, in the temple at Jerusalem (which is the last time Joseph is mentioned), but before Jesus was thirty, beginning his ministry. During Jesus' ministry, Mary and Jesus' brothers and sisters are mentioned, but not Joseph. Jesus, while on the cross, asks John to take care of his mother. Mary goes to John's house after Jesus' death rather than being cared for by her husband (John 19:26-27). However, perhaps Joseph merely died young.

Jesus is called a carpenter's son, (Matthew 13:55), so I have assumed Joseph was strong and fit enough for his trade and the flight to Egypt. Even if he were a little older than Mary he could not have been a frail man. For the purposes of this book I've assumed that Joseph is a little older, but not much.

What was Nazareth like?

It was in the north of Judah, a distance from Jerusalem in the south, and it was a small, agricultural village, with maybe 450 people living there.

Which flowers grow in Israel?

Blue irises and chamomile, certainly. For a guide to Israel and Palestine's flora, check out Biblewalks.com and www.flowers-israel-net.

How would they have travelled to Bethlehem?

I'm imagining that Mary at least went by donkey, rather than walking, but it would have been a long and difficult journey. Bethlehem, up in the hill country, was c. 70-90 miles away from the relatively low-lying Nazareth. They were unlikely to have gone through the enemy-country of Samaria as they wouldn't have been welcome or had anywhere to stay. They probably travelled east, crossing over the Jordan into Decapolis, and back through into Judea, thus bypassing Samaria. For a healthy person this would have taken three days of walking; in Mary's condition, I estimate it would have taken a week.

Were Mary and Joseph rejected by Joseph's family at Bethlehem?

I realise that my interpretation of events is a far-cry from the typical children's nativity interactions with a grumpy innkeeper. The reason I have chosen this scenario is because:

1. The word 'inn' can be translated 'guest room'. According to I. Howard Marshall[27] and Paula Gooder,[28] the latter is the preferred translation, because inns tended to be found on stretches of road, not in towns themselves, where you would expect hospitality.

2. Joseph lived in Nazareth, but his family line was in Bethlehem. It is therefore extremely unlikely that he would not have had any family already living in Bethlehem, and they would be the natural choice for hospitality. Why didn't they then receive him, when Mary was pregnant and about to give birth? In a hospitality culture, no matter how full the city was, or how many soldiers had commandeered the bedrooms, it is almost unthinkable that they wouldn't have been welcomed in by family. Possibly Joseph and Mary hadn't quite reached Bethlehem when Mary gave birth, forcing them into a nearby shelter. Alternatively, which is what I have supposed, Mary was rejected by Joseph's family because of the questions around Jesus' conception.

---

[27] I. Howard Marshall, *The Gospel of Luke, New International Greek Testament Commentary*, Eerdmans, 1996
[28] Paula Gooder, *Journey to the Manger*, Canterbury Press, 2015

Was Jesus born in a cave?

We don't know - neither a cave nor a stable is mentioned, only a manger (i.e. an animal's feeding trough). Some have supposed it was the courtyard room in a typical house where the fire would have been. Some have speculated that it was a stable or shed; some have thought it was an open-air field. From the second century, there has been a strong tradition that Jesus was born in a cave. Marshall points out that caves were sometimes used to shelter animals, like a garage, nearby the house. This is the theory that seemed most attractive and likely to me, so I opted for this one for my retelling.

Did Mary experience pain in labour?

Most Christians believe that we have 'original sin', inherited from Adam and Eve, and as a consequence we all carry the curses of their sin (listed in Genesis 3), including pain in labour. However, some Christians believe that Mary did not carry original sin. Within that tradition, some Christians therefore argue she was spared the pain of labour. As the Bible text doesn't specify, I felt free to go either way on this issue. I wanted to portray her as someone vulnerable, poor, weak and experiencing pain in labour, just as later Christ would hang on the cross as a criminal - poor, weak and experiencing pain. These are the main reasons behind this interpretative choice.

APPENDIX B
BIBLE STUDIES

Six Guided Discussions
for Small Groups

1. **THE WAIT OF THE WORLD**

   Being Patient - James 5:7-11

2. **SARAH**

   Scarred Souls and Hospitable Hearts - Genesis 18:1-15

3. **ISAIAH**

   How Long, O Lord? - Isaiah 6:1-13

4. **JOHN**

   Receiving Your Life as a Gift - John 3:22-30

5. **MARY**

   Belonging and Isolation - Luke 1:39-55

6. **THE GOD WHO WAITS**

   We Do Not Groan Alone - Romans 8:18-28

How to use the Bible Studies

The Bible Studies are designed to be used by groups over a six-week period in conjunction with *Those Who Wait*. In the week before each meeting, group members should read the relevant chapters, as follows:

Week One

~ **Individual pre-reading:** The Wait of the World
~ **Group study:** Being Patient - James 5:7-11

Week Two

~ **Individual pre-reading:** Sarah's Story
~ **Group study:** Scarred Souls and Hospitable Hearts - Genesis 18:1-15

Week Three

~ **Individual pre-reading:** Isaiah's Story
~ **Group study:** How Long, O Lord? - Isaiah 6:1-13

Week Four

~ **Individual pre-reading:** John's Story
~ **Group study:** Receiving Your Life as a Gift - John 3:22-30

Week Five

~ **Individual pre-reading:** Mary's Story
~ **Group study:** Belonging and Isolation - Luke 1:39-55

Week Six

~ **Individual pre-reading:** Epilogue: The God Who Waits
~ **Group study:** We Do Not Groan Alone - Romans 8:18-28

Welcome to the six group creative Bible discussions on the theme of waiting. These group sessions can stand alone, but you'll get the most out of them if you're reading the book alongside. The first session introduces the theme of waiting in patience. Group studies 2-5 follow the lives of Sarah, Isaiah, John the Baptist and Mary and use a passage relevant to their story. The final session ties the whole book together.

The studies will contain a variety of interactive Bible readings, Bible study questions, reflections, prayer and creative exercises, and a music option for quiet reflection.

The questions

The questions for Bible study are meant to be asked in the order they're given, but the suggestions for music, creative exercises and prayer ideas are designed to be a menu, for the leader to select what would best fit the group in the time available.

There are no theological notes or 'answers' for the questions, partly because I've tried to ask questions that are either straightforward in the text or don't have a right answer.

Group values

Many of the Bible study questions are personal and designed to foster deeper honesty, so use discretion if you don't know the others in your group well.

At their best, Bible study groups reflect a safe place to be honest. Confidentiality rules can help, along with providing a safe and loving space for people to share difficult life experiences.

Being Patient - James 5:7-11

Pre-reading:

From the Introduction chapters, read 'The Wait of the World'.

Props required for leaders:

~ the Bible passage printed out for each person
~ blank sheets of paper and pens for everyone for the Clock exercise

Pray as you start

1. On a scale of 1-10 (10 being excellent, 1 being awful), how good would you say you are at waiting?

The Clock - What are you waiting for?

On a blank piece of paper, draw a small clock.

Think about all the areas of your life where you feel 'liminal': in-between, unfulfilled, in limbo. (Look back through the suggestions in the Introduction Chapters if you need a prompt.)

Around the clock, write down everything in your life that you are waiting for, from the 'little waitings' to the 'big waits'.

This can be a surprisingly vulnerable exercise.

Share with others (as much as you feel comfortable) about the big and little things you're waiting for.

Keep this clock somewhere prominent as you work through this book, as a reminder of all you're waiting for, and refer to it in subsequent Bible study discussions.

Setting the scene

In this first study, we will look at a few verses from James, considering how our lives are currently marked by waiting, and the value of patience. The author of the letter is traditionally understood to be James, the brother of Jesus, writing to Jewish Christians in the early church who were undergoing trials.

Read aloud: James 5:7-11

2. James urges his fellow believers to be patient as they wait for the Lord. He was referring to the return of Jesus at the end of time. How often do you find yourself thinking about heaven or Jesus' return? Why do you think this is?

    Note: Although James is talking predominantly about waiting for Jesus' return, we can also apply the points below in terms of waiting for Jesus to 'come' into and make right the situations we're in.

3. Think about the metaphor of the farmer in verse 7. A farmer prepares the ground, sows the seed, waits for the rain, watches the crop slowly take shape, harvests the crop, and stores seed to plant the following year. Which of these steps best describe where you are in your waiting?

4. Looking at verse 9 - note that James doesn't tell them here not to grumble about the situation they're in, but urges them not to attack each other while they wait. How can we avoid attacking others when we are stressed with uncertainty?

5. Looking at verses 10-11 - remember that the prophets who spoke in the name of the Lord faced opposition, sometimes didn't see their prophecies fulfilled, felt ridiculed, isolated and often questioned God. They waited messily. Which words stand out for you as encouragements here?

6. From this passage, find something you want to cling to in this journey of conscious waiting. How can you prophetically speak this into your life as you wait? Perhaps there's a verse or phrase you could memorise or doodle for a minute. As you read the passage, perhaps God will give you an image or picture that you want to record. Perhaps write over your 'clock' one word or phrase that stands out.

    Take a moment to do this prayerfully, then share with others the word or phrase, with as much explanation as you want to give. This week, whenever you feel frustrated with waiting, aim to recall it.

Summary

> "Be patient, then, brothers and sisters, until the Lord's coming."
> James 5:7

James was thinking specifically about Christ's future return when he spoke to his Christian community. However, it can also apply to the different ways Christ 'comes' to us in our circumstances. James encourages his readers not to attack one another as they face difficult circumstances but to be patient like a farmer, knowing that there will be good fruit one day even though the seed seems inactive. He urges them to remember the prophets and how they waited for Christ, which is what we will be doing in the rest of the book.

Pray

Ask for prayer about the situations you face, as much as you feel comfortable sharing. If you found a helpful image or word, incorporate that into your prayers. Invite God into your waiting as you start this journey.

You might like to read the prayer below together.

A Prayer Suggestion for Those Who Wait

Dear Lord, I am waiting [to/for]
[pause to name aloud or silently the waiting situation you shared in the clock exercise].

You came to earth as a weak human.
You will come again in glory as a powerful King.
In between these times,
Please come afresh into my life.
I invite you into my frustration, my excitement;
My disappointment, my hope.

Let me know your empathy as a God-born-baby;
In control of the universe, yet helpless and flailing.
Let me know your power as a good ruler
Who acts at just the right time and comes to make everything right.
Remind me of the good beginning and the good ending.

Lord, be with me in the middle of my story.
Bring me perspective, and let me see your purpose in the waiting.

While I wait, give me endurance and strength to hold fast to you.
Lord Jesus Christ, would you come to me today.
Amen

HOMEWORK - Creative Exercise - The Practice of Waiting:

For however long it takes you to work through this book, whenever you find yourself waiting, (perhaps for an appointment or in a traffic jam), try not to pick up your phone or book; don't distract yourself at all. Instead, sit with the silence and the discomfort awhile. Aim to spend at least fifteen minutes pausing each day, even if your day feels full.
~   What do you feel when you wait like this?
~   What does it tell you about yourself? And about God?
Invite God into those conscious times of waiting. Perhaps God will speak, perhaps there will be silence - what matters is making space.

Breath-prayers for Seasons of Waiting

Use these as prayers for when you can't pray, those moments when your deferred dreams are too much to handle. Pray these as often as you need in the days or weeks that you work through this book.

~   "Please, Lord, be with me in the waiting, be present in my confusion."
~   "O Lord, lift up my head."
~   "Spirit, please take my burden."
~   "Lord Jesus, refresh my hope and give me peace."
~   "I wait for the Lord, my whole being waits; and in his word I put my hope." (Psalm 130:5)
~   "Lord, I wait for you; you will answer, Lord my God." (Psalm 38:15)

Scarred Souls and Hospitable Hearts - Genesis 18:1-15

Pre-reading:

Sarah's Story in *Those Who Wait.*

Props required for leaders:

~ Blank paper, for making a comparison chart between Abraham and Sarah
~ Blank paper for love letters
~ Stone and pens for writing on stones
~ A book with names and origins, or a similar website, such as Behindthename.com/search.php
~ Blindfold
~ **Music:** Recordings of traditional Advent hymns that focus on waiting, not nativity

Pray as you start

1. If God were to pop round uninvited to your house, what meal would you serve?

Setting the Scene

We've followed Sarah's journey as she waited for God's promise to be fulfilled. Today we're returning to one of those incidents and putting it under the magnifying glass. We'll contrast her response with Abraham's, exploring the grace of God to all in the process of waiting.

Read aloud Genesis 18:1-15

2. Looking at verses 1-8, God shows up at the most inconvenient time - the heat of the day, when everyone wants to be sleeping, not rushing around. What are the ways Abraham shows hospitality? List them on the left side of the page.

3. Now focus on verses 9-15. While Abraham is doing this, how does Sarah respond? List all the things she does on the right side of the page.

4. Looking at verses 1-15, what do you observe about the differences between them?

5. Abraham reacts to the visitors with extravagant hospitality and openness, whereas Sarah is more hidden away. Sarah's reticence could be explained by her role in society to be submissive and not talk to men, or it could be a spiritual or emotional reason. To what extent do you see yourself in either of their responses to the Lord's visit?

6. We might think that Abraham would be rewarded and Sarah chided or punished. But focus on what the Lord says in verses 9, 10 and 13-15. How does the Lord show love and concern for Sarah, not just Abraham?

7. Genesis 21:1, when Sarah gives birth, says, "Now the Lord was gracious to Sarah as he had said, and the Lord did for Sarah what he had promised". What does God's relationship with Sarah tell us about God's character?

Summary

Sarah's life journey shows us that God is gracious, not just to the hopeful Abrahams of the world, but to bitter and disappointed people. God was determined to bless Sarah, no matter what her response was to Him. God keeps his promises, even when we're too defeated by disappointment to believe them anymore.

Clothing ourselves in cynicism often makes the pain more bearable. But God sees through our cynicism and pain, and invites us to trust him once more.

8. How has your own history with God over the years influenced your response to God during a period of waiting (either positively or negatively)?

9. What might you learn from someone who has had the opposite experience?

10. Abraham worked hard to make his home hospitable to God, even though God came at a difficult time. In a similar way, this can inspire us to cultivate hospitable hearts towards God, to be open and ready to receive or hear from him. How can you make your heart more open and welcoming towards God?

We often want a clear reason for God delaying good things. We want to know the reason why. Sarah's story doesn't give us a clear reason. Instead, Sarah's life tells us that:

a) we should follow the guidance God is giving us, even though it looks strange;

b) God has not forgotten us;

c) God honours us;

d) God wants us to trust again;

e) God longs to bring us joy.

11. As you think about your own journey with waiting, which of these five truths about God do you need to remember or truly believe for yourself? As you think about supporting others in their journey of waiting, which truths could you share or pray over them?

Pray

God loves both Abrahams and Sarahs, and we need each other. Pray for and encourage one another in our different situations, remembering God's grace to all.

Choose one or two from these Creative Exercises

Creative Exercise: Name change

God changed Abram and Sarai's names, just subtly, to encourage their spirits so that they would pause and remember God.

If you could imagine God changing your name through this process of conscious waiting, what name would you hope God gave you? (You might use a baby name book, or a website where you can search for the meaning and find a name, e.g. Behindthename.com/search.php.) Write that new name on a stone and keep it as a reminder of hope.

Creative Exercise: Walking in the dark

If you are able, have someone blindfold you and lead you around, without telling you where you are going or when they will stop. How does it feel to be led in this way? To what extent do you think this is how Sarah and Abraham felt? To what extent does your relationship with God feel like this? Whatever your feelings and reflections on this experience, turn them into prayer.

Creative Exercise: Love letter from God (either take ten minutes during the group time, or do as 'homework')

After you have looked back through the last year, consider writing an affirming love letter to yourself, as though it were God writing to you. What does he think about you? What does he want to say to you about this year? What does he want you to remember?

This is what I imagine such a love letter might look like if God were writing to Sarah:

Dear Sarah,

I know you think I've forgotten you and that I don't see you, I just see Abraham. The truth is I love you and value you very much. Remember the time in Egypt, when Abraham behaved so appallingly? I was angry that he dishonoured you and abandoned you.

I want you to know that I will never do that to you. I am here for you. I know it's hard for you to trust me right now, because it's been so many years and you still haven't had a baby. I know it's your heart's desire, and how unbearable it is for you to wait. I know you thought that it would solve things for Hagar to have a baby, and it hasn't; it's made it worse. I know all this, and I love you through it all.

I'm asking you to wait a little longer. I know it's tough, but I'm hoping you can find me in the waiting. I'm here, and I love you very much. You are so precious to me, and I delight in you. I see you, even when so many others don't. Keep going.

With much love, God

What would your love letter from God say? Take some time, go to a place where you feel comfortable and have minimal distraction, and write that letter as though you were writing from God to you. If you need a template, replace the underlined parts with your experience.

Report Back: How does it feel to write it?

Music

Take some time this week to listen to an advent hymn about waiting for Jesus, e.g. Come, Thou Long Expected Jesus (Charles Wesley); Joy to the World, the Lord is Come (Isaac Watts); Lo, He Comes with Clouds Descending (Charles Wesley).

How Long, O Lord? - Isaiah 6:1-13

Pre-reading:

Isaiah's Story in *Those Who Wait*

Props required for leaders:

- ~ Passage printed out with space for doodling
- ~ Newspapers for creative exercise, scissors and glue
- ~ **Music:** Mozart's *Requiem*; Handel's *Messiah*

Pray as you start

Setting the scene

This study is a little different, as it focuses on an interactive Bible reading, rather than questions, to get into the story. Today we'll be looking closely at the time that Isaiah met God in the temple, and how meeting with God changes everything.

1. As you lift your eyes to look past your immediate situation to the world at large, which are the national and global situations about which you are anxious, longing for a good outcome? Write them out and then share.

Bible Reading: Isaiah 6:1-13

Read Isaiah 6:1-13 individually, with a pen and paper, or have someone **read through the text slowly.**

On the first reading:

As you listen to/read the passage, imagine yourself in the scene. Go there with your senses.

- ~ Who are you in the scene - God/cherubs/Isaiah - or something else?

~ Where are you in the scene?
~ What is your posture?
~ What do you feel?

Share your experience with others.

On the second reading:

As you listen to/read the passage, which one word or phrase stands out to you? Why? Take a while to roll it around your mind and absorb it. Consider how it speaks to your current situation and the world situations that concern you.

Share with others what your one word or phrase is.

Note:

For those who struggle with verse 10, it is worth noting that Paul had a different interpretation of Isaiah's words, saying that God foreknew their stubbornness, rather than foreordained it (see Acts 28:25-27).

Discussion Questions

Isaiah's calling was a strange one: to speak truth and warn of destruction - even when people wouldn't listen to him. He was to continue to speak a seemingly futile message, even as a nation sleepwalked into war. But he had the strength to speak that unpopular message because he had seen the spiritual reality of God on the throne.

2. Thinking about your immediate circle of family and friends and also wider society, in which situations can you relate to Isaiah's calling to speak an urgent message of truth to which no one listens?

3. Isaiah's commission focused on national and global issues. Although God cares about us as individuals, it's easy to forget that most of the Bible focuses on communities, nations, peoples: the plural, rather than the singular. When you pray, where on the spectrum between personal concerns and world issues would you say your focus was? Do you feel you have the balance right?

4. As we look around our world, there is much to discourage us, just as there was much to discourage Isaiah as he met with God in the temple. But reading further in Isaiah's life, we see many mercies to the nation of Judah - like God protecting Jerusalem from Assyria's attack because Hezekiah prayed for help (2 Kings 18-19). God turns quickly

to help those who ask. How does this and Isaiah's vision of God on the throne encourage you this week?

In Isaiah 1-11, we see God's:

- ~ awesome power as the Ruler on the throne,
- ~ concern for the vulnerable in society,
- ~ anger at empty religion used as a cover to disregard God's laws, and
- ~ relentless commitment and grace to an unreliable people.

5. Which of these, or other truths about God from the passage, do you need to hold today?

6. Take a moment to that truth into an image, either in your head or on paper, and try to hold that image in your head this week as a basis for prayer. What image do you have?

Summary

It's hard to live in the tension of what is and what could be. We want a control switch for the bigger issues that fill us with helplessness, so that everything is made right. We want to fast-forward to Isaiah's vision of world peace.

Instead, God tells us to:
a) *grieve* and lament over the injustice in the world and in our own hearts;
b) *speak* the truth, even when no one is listening and it feels pointless;
c) *live* out the calling to be a truth-teller;
d) *look* to God for future hope and present leadership.

7. As you think about the wrongs in the world today, which of these four options seems to be what God is asking from you right now?

Bring to God in prayer your uncertainty about your own life and the world at large.

Music

'Dies Irae' from Mozart's *Requiem* has a wonderful juxtaposition between the furious music of the 'Dies irae, dies illa' (day of anger, day of judgement) parts and the mournful cry of 'Salva me' (a plea for salvation).

Listen to the lesser-known air from Handel's *Messiah*, 'The people who walked in darkness', followed by the more famous, 'For unto us a child is born'. As you listen, meditate on or worship Jesus.

Newspaper exercise - A meditation on Isaiah 3-5

Chapters 3-5 of Isaiah detail the reasons that judgement was coming not only to Assyria, but to Judah as well. The leaders (predominantly men) are guilty of 'grinding the faces of the poor' while the rich women flaunt their wealth in the trinkets they wear and the goods they own (see Isaiah 3:14-26). It is not hard to recognise our own world today in this picture.

Today, take some newspapers and magazines plus two large sheets of paper. Each time you come across a news story associated with oppression or injustice, paste it on one sheet. Every time you come across an advert for something to buy, put it on the other sheet.

- ~ How do these two pieces of paper, side by side, spark prayer in you for your society; the church; yourself?
- ~ What do you need to change in your thoughts, behaviour, or lifestyle to better reflect the heart of God?

Review

How are you doing with the discipline of conscious waiting, spending a little time each day waiting? What does it feel like to lean into the discomfort of waiting?

Prayer suggestion - Praying Psalm 13

Use this psalm as a basis for your prayer, personalising the words underlined, as appropriate. Spend time writing what your situations would be. Share them, as you feel comfortable, with the rest of the group. Then, as a leader reads out all but the underlined words, speak aloud (as you feel comfortable sharing) your own prayers to God in the silences.

For the director of music. A psalm of David.

How long, Lord? Will you forget me for ever?
　　How long will you hide your face from me?
How long must I wrestle with my thoughts
　　and day after day have sorrow in my heart?
　　How long will my enemy triumph over me?
[name the situations you worry about]

Look on me and answer, Lord my God.
　Give light to my eyes, or I will sleep in death,
and my enemy will say, 'I have overcome him,'
　and my foes will rejoice when I fall.
[name the possible consequences if God doesn't intervene]

But I trust in your unfailing love;
　my heart rejoices in your salvation.
I will sing the Lord's praise,
　for he has been good to me.

Receiving Your Life as a Gift - John 3:22-30

Pre-reading:

John's Story in *Those Who Wait*

Props required for leaders:

~ Passage printed out onto paper and pens for all members.
~ Blank paper
~ **Music:** recording of O Come, O Come Emmanuel; Handel's *Messiah*

Props required for members:

~ Two objects of value in some way to you.

Pray as you start

1. Thinking back to school plays and sports teams; awards or roles; can you recall a time when you didn't get the part or position you wanted? Were you ever jealous of someone else?

Setting the Scene

As we enter John's story today, we're at the point after Jesus' baptism, but before John has been imprisoned. Jesus had also been baptising, but whereas John baptised as a ceremony of Jewish repentance, Jesus is proposing something new: being born of water and Spirit, and being baptised as a sign of commitment to Jesus. How would this affect John and his ministry of baptism? We find out in this study.

Read John 3:22-30, listening out for repeated words or themes.

2. Read the whole passage, especially verses 26-28. What evidence do we see that John's disciples wanted to make John their messiah?

3. Jesus was The Messiah: God's chosen one to make the world right again; God himself, born as a baby. But we can sometimes be tempted to forget this, and make other people our 'messiah' instead. We look to them for leadership and rescue, rather than to Jesus. When you consider your life right now, to what extent do you feel like John's disciples, desperate to make your favourite person your 'messiah'?

4. Which 'messiahs' do you need to lay down in order to refocus on Jesus? Share as you feel comfortable.

5. Review verses 22-26 - what reasons did John have for being jealous of Jesus?

6. Think through your life at the moment. In which areas of your life do you envy others?

7. Looking at verses 28-29 - how does John describe his role? And how does he feel about it?

8. Looking at verses 27-30 - what is admirable about John's response?

9. Looking at verse 27 - How does it feel to view your life and work as things you've 'received' from God, rather than earned or created?

Summary

John lived as the eternal best man or bridesmaid. His focus was always on Jesus and glorifying him. His whole life was focused on waiting for Christ, and he faithfully played his role in that, being careful not to seek glory himself. It challenges us similarly.

10. How does John's life and attitude speak to you and into your circumstances today?

Creative Exercise: Waiting for Your Calling

A calling is not just something related to Christian ministry but can be defined as something you feel you were made to do - that thing that makes you feel alive (we'll call this 'Plan A' calling). For me, that would be church ministry; writing; speaking; broadcasting; spiritual mentoring; training leaders; pastoral care for writers and church leaders. What would yours be?

However, a calling can also be defined as something that you struggle with but that God has asked of you to do. For me, that is spending a lot of time resting. For my husband, it's spending a lot of time washing and cooking (we'll call this 'Plan B, C, D....Z' calling, depending on how it feels).

~ What is your 'Plan A' calling, if you know it?
~ What kind of calling(s) are you living with right now?
~ How has waiting played a part in that (or how is waiting playing a part in that)?
~ To what extent do you see God's grace in it all?
~ Share with others as you feel comfortable.

Now choose two valuable objects - one to represent the 'Plan A' life you wish you lived, and one to represent the 'Plan B...Z' life you are living. Lay them in front of you.

~ What does it feel like for both of these life options to be represented as valuable?
~ Between these two objects, where do you want to place your hands?
~ What do you want to do with the objects? Where do you want them to be?
~ Can you cradle them both in your hand?

Commit both your thankfulness and frustrated dreams together to God. Use these actions with the objects as a prayer to God, even if you don't have the words.

Music

This week, listen to O Come, O Come, Emmanuel (for a modern recording, try Enya, Sugarland or Pentatonix.) Also, from Handel's *Messiah*, 'Every valley shall be exalted' and 'Then shall the eyes of the blind be open'd'. While you listen, focus on Jesus as the Messiah - God's anointed leader.

Prayer

Look again through the passage. Pick a verse or phrase that stands out to you today, and take a moment to write or doodle it on a piece of paper. This week, put it somewhere you can see it. Use that verse or phrase now to centre your prayers, as you bring to God your frustrations, longings and temptation to envy.

Prayer Challenge

Having named situations or people you envy, pray - if you can - a prayer of blessing over them. Ask God to bless you, too.

GROUP STUDY 5
Mary's Story

Belonging and Isolation - Luke 1:39-55

Pre-reading:

Mary's Story in *Those Who Wait*

Props required for leaders:

- ~ Printouts of the passage for members, with pens for annotating
- ~ Blank paper and pens for Inside: Outside exercise
- ~ **Music:** The Magnificat, e.g. by Rutter or Helen Dennis.

Props required for members:

- ~ Your 'clock'

Pray as you start

1. Look back at your clock. Think about your longings and situations of waiting. In what ways do they make you feel ostracised, an outsider? Share with the group as you feel comfortable.

Setting the scene

We have seen through Mary's story the joy of Jesus' incarnation but also the pressures and dangers on her as she waited for his birth. As we zoom in on the meeting of Mary and Elizabeth, we will focus on Mary's song and how it speaks of God's love for the forgotten in society.

To open up the passage, we will do an **interactive reading** together.

2. Read aloud Luke 1:39-55, and as you do, envisage yourself in the scene.

- Who are you in the scene - Mary, Elizabeth, a mute Zechariah, unable to speak until his baby is born, other friends and neighbours?

- Are you rich or poor?

- In the centre or outside?

- What are you feeling and experiencing?

3. Read through the passage a second time. This time, listen out for one word or short phrase that speaks to your soul or most stands out to you. Close your eyes and listen, or use a pen to annotate a printed out copy. Share your word or phrase with others.

4. Looking at verses 39-45 - many people would not have believed Mary's miraculous story, which would have left her very vulnerable and ostracised from polite religious society. But Elizabeth, full of the Holy Spirit, spoke words over Mary not just of belonging, but of exaltation. Look over Elizabeth's words and actions to Mary. Which words or actions stand out for you?

5. Compare Mary's assent to Gabriel in Luke 1:38, 'May your word to me be fulfilled', with her outburst of joy here (verses 46-48). When in your life have you responded to God initially, 'okay, then', only to realise a little later than God has blessed you beyond measure?

6. Looking at verses 49-55 - take one highlighter or pen and circle all the words that talk about God's character (look for the 'He has' statements). What picture of God does this build?

7. Looking at verses 51-53 - identify the three 'reversals' here. How do you respond to reading these reversals - e.g. does it gladden or unsettle your heart?

8. 1 Peter describes our state as Christians as 'exiles and foreigners' - our home is heaven.[29] As far back as Sarah and Abraham, our spiritual ancestors were nomads, wanderers in the wilderness; our Saviour was a homeless drifter, born in an emergency shelter. We are not home yet: heaven is our true home. What difference does it make to have this perspective about our Christian journey?

---

[29] 1 Peter 1:1, 2:11

9. **Sarah and Abraham** were on the outskirts of society, with Sarah in disgrace for most of her life for being childless.

   Isaiah spoke against the status quo, which made him unpopular.

   John spent his life in the desert or in prison, away from the centre of civilisation.

   Mary lived with a question mark of propriety over her life and morals, despite being utterly obedient to God and honoured by God.

   How does their disgrace and isolation encourage or challenge us, either generally as Christians, or in our situations of waiting?

10. God gave Mary a friendship with Elizabeth at a crucial time of waiting. Who are your 'Elizabeths'? To whom can you be a friend like Elizabeth was to Mary?

Summary

The Lord showed kindness to Mary by giving her Elizabeth to allay any doubts and to encourage, protect and prepare her for her important role. God loves the outsider, and loves to lift those who are down. The Lord still shows kindness to those who are in need. We need eyes to see people from God's viewpoint, not the world's.

Music

Listen to a version of The Magnificat (Mary's song, 'My soul magnifies the Lord...'). Classical recordings abound: for longer pieces try Vivaldi, CPE Bach, JC Bach, or Rutter; for more contemporary pieces try My Soul Magnifies by Helen Dennis. As you listen to Mary's song of thanksgiving, consider the ways you have been included by God. Give thanks for 'Elizabeths' in your life who encourage you.

Creative Exercise: Inside / Outside

~ Often, in a time of waiting, we can feel like we are on the outside of things.
~ On a piece of paper, list all the ways you feel ostracised or that you don't belong. Write the names of as many Bible characters you know who also fit those categories or in some way didn't belong.

~ Draw a big circle round all these longings, as though it is Jesus' arms embracing you.
~ Spend some time thinking of how Jesus treated outsiders, and imagine him with you.
~ Spend time in prayer, perhaps mourning the ways you don't belong, or thanking God for the ways you're included.
~ As you pray, picture God's powerful, merciful, loving arms around you.
~ Pray for anyone else who feels ostracised or isolated.

We Do Not Groan Alone – Romans 8:18-28

Pre-reading:

Epilogue: The God Who Waits

Props required for leaders:

~ Printouts of the passage with coloured pens for all members
~ Your 'clock'
~ **Music:** I surrender all (e.g. Robin Marks, Libbi, Casting Crowns)

Props required for members:

~ Bring an object or picture that represents your longing and everything you're waiting for.

Pray as you start

1. When, as a child or adult, were you glad of someone with you in a scary situation?

Setting the scene

Whenever we're in difficult situations, it's good to know we're not alone. For the last five sessions, we have been on a journey through the lives of followers of God who waited imperfectly. As we consider how we wait and what we still long for, we delve into Romans 8. Paul's letter to the Christians in Rome gives us comfort and reassurance in our struggles with waiting.

Read aloud Romans 8:18-28

As someone reads the passage, take coloured pens and mark in different colours repeated themes and words on the printouts. Doodle, underline the things that stand out for you, put a question mark where things puzzle you, and an exclamation mark where things surprise you. Take a couple of minutes to look over the passage in silence once it's read.

2. What do you notice as you look at this passage afresh? Share your observations and questions with one another.

3. Look at verses 19, 23 and 26, which mention creation, ourselves and the Spirit groaning, as we wait for Christ to return. What difference does it make to you to picture your frustrations as part of a larger picture, with God and creation partaking in your struggle?

Read aloud the passage again and this time, listen out for all the occasions it mentions hope or something positive in the future.

4. To what extent do these hopes ring true for you?

5. What is your favourite verse from this passage? Share with others why this is, and doodle it on your paper. This week, try to memorise it.

Looking back at *Those Who Wait*

6. Which character most resonated with you? Why is this?

7. As you think over these stories, what most surprised you?

8. How have these stories taught you about waiting?

9. In which ways have you encountered God through this book?

The Clock

Revisit the picture of the clock, and consider all those areas of your life in which you feel 'liminal': in-between, unfulfilled, in limbo.

~ Over the past few weeks, as you've spent time sitting with the discomfort of waiting, what have you discovered through this practice?

~ In what ways, if any, has your approach to waiting changed?

~ Which prayers, if any, have been answered?

~ Overall, what have you gained from this journey?

Summary

In many ways, *Those Who Wait* is an extended meditation on these verses Paul wrote to encourage the Roman Christians in the first century AD. We long for heaven, we are waiting for wholeness, and in the meantime, we groan. But we are not alone. As we sit with our longings, we remember that God is with us, advocates for us and is working to bring good. The main application of these verses is the act of remembering.

10. As you live in the now-and-not-yet of God's kingdom, what will you do to remember that God is with you in the waiting?

Music

'I surrender all - All to Jesus' - there's a simple recording by Robin Mark of this hymn or a one-verse acoustic version by Libbi. (Casting Crowns do a modern tune.) Play the song or read aloud the lyrics, and these words as a prayer for your own life.

A prayer of hope (with other people)

~ Choose an object, perhaps something in your house, that represents something of your longing. Feel the object in your hands: the weight and the shape of it.

~ How tightly do you want to hold onto it? How do you feel when you hold it?

~ Feel the weight of holding it alone. Then, if you are comfortable, others can cup their hands around yours, hold the object with you and join you in prayer specifically for that situation.

Select Bibliography

The Anchor Bible Dictionary on CD-ROM. Logos Research Systems, 2002.

Childs, Brevard S. *Isaiah.* Westminster John Knox Press, 2001.

Dapaah, Daniel S. *The Relationship between John the Baptist and Jesus of Nazareth: a Critical Study.* University Press of America, 2005.

Gooder, Paula. *Journey to the Manger: Exploring the Birth of Jesus.* Canterbury Press, 2015.

Gooder, Paula. *The Meaning Is in the Waiting: the Spirit of Advent.* Canterbury Press, 2008.

Gordon, Charlotte. *The Woman Who Named God: Abraham's Dilemma and the Birth of Three Faiths.* Little, Brown, 2009.

Marshall, I. Howard. *The Gospel of Luke: a Commentary on the Greek Text, NIGTC.* William B. Eerdmans, 1996.

Oswalt, John N. *The Book of Isaiah: Chapters 1-39, NICOT.* Vol. 1, Eerdmans, 1986.

Reid, Daniel G. *The IVP Dictionary of the New Testament: a One-Volume Compendium of Contemporary Biblical Scholarship.* InterVarsity Press, 2004.

Seuss, Dr. *Oh, the Places You'll Go!* Random House, 1990.

Williams, Jenni. *God Remembered Rachel: Women's Stories in the Old Testament and Why They Matter.* SPCK, 2014.

Wolf, Herbert M. "A Solution to the Immanuel Prophecy in Isaiah 7:14-8:22." *Journal of Biblical Literature*, vol. 91, no. 4, 1972, p. 449., doi:10.2307/3263678.

Young, Amy. *Looming Transitions: Starting and Finishing Well in Cross-Cultural Service.* CreateSpace Independent Publishing Platform, 2016.

Author's Acknowledgements

They say it takes a village to write a book. I reckon this one took a sprawling metropolis. I'll do my best to remember everyone...

Inspirers

In terms of inspiration for the book, I stand on the shoulders of giants:

Paula Gooder - I'm so grateful for your exegesis in *The Meaning Is in the Waiting*. *Journey to the Manger* helped me work through some of the tricky questions of the nativity. Thank you for your work.

John Blase - *Touching Wonder* was such a work of beauty that it made me cry. I am no poet, but your poetry inspired my prose. Likewise, Ed Cyzewski's storytelling abilities in *The Good News of Revelation* moved me profoundly and highlighted the drama of the New Testament. Thank you to Andrew Goddard for that St Andrew's sermon that was pure storytelling, and Alice Buckley, who gave me permission to play. All of you opened my eyes to teaching the Bible narratively and playfully.

Pete Greig - I will always be grateful for *God on Mute*, for many, many reasons. Thanks for your honesty and theology on the silences of God and unanswered prayer.

Early Days

Thank you to Cara Strickland, dear friend, cheerleader and food writer *par excellence*, who saw the value in my tentative experiments, and cheered me on in this genre when I thought no one was reading it. Thank you to Mark Arnold and Sean Doherty for quick Old Testament consultation in the early stages, and Ros, for being Ros. Thanks to Ruth Cooper, Dominique Van Werkhoven and Rachel Bedford who affirmed early versions and boosted my confidence. Simon Cox and Becki Bradshaw - thanks for your encouragement in the value of this book at a key time.

Thank you to Beth Morey, Tara Owens and Amy Young who were my on-hand emergency geniuses (or should that be genii?) to help with some of the creative exercises.

Thank you to the 2015/16 Beta Readers, who helped shape this book and provided such valuable feedback: Tracey Layman, Tanya Thiessen, Cat Caird, Janice DeFluiter, Amanda Chapman, Kathryn MacFarlane, Jean Vann, Trece Wyman, Betsy Blatchley, Pam Smith, Cecilia Milburn, Carol Newnham, Nay Dawson, Rachel Watson, Mary Beth Pavlik, Dom and

Rachel, Steffy B, Lizzie Watson, Shona Minson, Abby Norman, Jenn LeBow, Gayl Wright, Nicole Romero, Jamie Bonilla.

The Book's Midwives

Amy Boucher Pye - you spotted this book as a diamond in the rough, and you helped me realise its potential. If it wasn't for you, this book wouldn't be here. You are an incredible advocate, adviser and friend, and I am so grateful to God for you. Thank you for your wisdom and discernment - and for blue toenails.

Alice Buckley - thank you for being my running partner in this crazy journey called writing, for the debates on who would play me in the movie of my life and for always saying the perfect thing. Blood sisters forever, dude.

Steffy DooDah - thanks for knitted lemurs, free therapy sessions, beautiful poetry and for not showing me spiders. Shona Minson - thanks for your inspirational pomodoro-ing and for always being honest. Amy Young - you bring such rich wisdom and joy to every conversation we have, and I want to be like you when I grow up. Abby Norman - you are always my kindred spirit adopted sister, and you *know* me; Beth Morey - you have calmed and encouraged me - thanks for all your support for the book and my life in general. Tara Owens, Esther Emery, Jamie Bonilla - you are always inspiring me.

Vicky Beeching - I'm so grateful for our decades-long friendship and the ways we live parallel lives. Thanks for walking with me in the worlds of book-writing and chronic illness, and for completely understanding the necessity of obsessive lipstick research. You rock!

Cat Caird - thank you for being someone who models to me what patience looks like - not least when I vomit my news all over you whilst I'm still trying to remember whether I was looking for coffee or milk.

Janice DeFluiter, Amy Young, Mary Beth Pavlik - you are magical editing fairies who apparated when I needed you most. Ali Ryder - thanks for last-minute help. Addie - you wrote the most perfect foreword; you understand my heart so well. Ed Cyzewski - I am stunned by how you champion me and others with such generosity. Thank you so much for your time and wisdom.

Dearest Wellies - I would be lost without you. Thank you for sustaining me in so many ways, honouring my angst, and for being with me through my writing journey. I wouldn't be a writer without you. I don't have the words to say how grateful I am for you. Thank you, thank you, thank you.

Thank you to my lovely book club and clergy wives group for keeping me sane over the years. There were too many to name, but thank you to all my eagle-eyes in the launch team. Thank you to early reviewers and my endorsers for cheering me on. A big thank you to Sheila Marlow for copy-editing services that went above and beyond.

Laura Ferguson - if I could make anyone a patron saint of graphic designers, I would choose you. Thank you for your beautiful design, and for sacrificing precious mama-sleep while we talked typefaces. You are utterly wonderful.

Malcolm Down - thank you for taking a chance on this new author and for all your help and support in getting this book into the world. Thanks for going the extra mile in multiple ways. You are a publisher who genuinely believes in bringing untold stories to life, and you've been a dream to work with. Chloe Evans, thanks for saving me embarrassment.

Family and more

Thank you to St Pancras Church for loving me even when I can't give anything, and for being incredibly supportive to us as a family. When people ask me what a good, loving church looks like, I describe you.

Jenny Rowbory - thank you for helping me keep this book true. I am deeply indebted to you for your friendship, prayer and care of me. Here's to your perseverance in the face of extreme suffering - and jolly japes, JK Rowling and Dr Awesome. Oy, with the poodles already! I wish you all the joy of a thousand penguins slip-sliding their way into the sea.

Thank you to Mum and Dad M, who look after us so well, in so many ways. Thank you for caring for me at a crucial time, and for doing so with such love, patience and paleo cooking.

A big thank you to Mum and Dad for enthusiastically endorsing my books ever since I was seven and wrote that Enid Blyton rip-off with bad illustrations. Thanks for crafting my subtitle with me and recommending my books to everyone you know. I should pay you commission! (I won't.) Thank you for your love and celebration of me and my writing.

To my gorgeous angel boy - thank you for loving books, writing your own books alongside me and daily delighting me with puns. You have the best laugh in the world, and I love you.

And to Jon, who has always made me laugh just at the point when I feel I will explode: thank you for not exploding during this process. Thank you for motivational mantras, continually telling me to just write the actual book, for beautiful art that expresses the heartbeat of this work, for all your behind-the-scenes effort in making it happen - and for reading it! Thanks for being generally Jesus-y. I'm so glad you're my husband.

Above all, thank you God, the Holy Trinity, for always showing up in the wilderness, for grace in weakness and for fresh mercies every morning. I love you, Lord.

And you! Thank you, dear reader, for accompanying me on this creative journey on the theme of waiting in the Bible.

Do keep in touch - sign up to my newsletter for writing-related and personal updates, exclusive offers and a FREE gift. Go to tanyamarlow.com for more details or simply enter your details here: tinyurl.com/tanyamarlowwaits

What did you think of this book?

If you could leave a short, honest review on Amazon, Goodreads and whichever store you bought it from, this makes any author *beyond* happy. If you loved it, you could mention it on your social media outlets, talk about it to your friends or recommend it at conferences and church. It makes a huge difference to new authors. Thank you!

More from Tanya Marlow

Coming Back to God When You Feel Empty - Tanya Marlow

How do you find a path back to faith when you're feeling empty? Marlow interweaves her own story of loss and homecoming with the biblical book of Ruth, providing a path back to God after disappointment and loss. At fifty pages, it's a short read for busy people.

About the Author

Formerly a lecturer in Biblical Theology and in church ministry for over a decade, **Tanya Marlow** is now a writer, speaker and broadcaster on faith and spirituality.

Her books include *Those Who Wait: Finding God in disappointment, doubt and delay* and *Coming Back to God When You Feel Empty*.

Despite being housebound with Myalgic Encephalomyelitis (ME), she is a popular speaker at churches and Christian conferences (via video link). She has also appeared on BBC Radio 4 and BBC Spotlight (TV), and her writing has been published by *The Spectator, Relevant Magazine, Premier Christianity* and more.

She campaigns for those with chronic illness and disability, and for medical equality for ME patients, volunteering with #MEAction Network.

She was born in Kent, fell in love in Durham and got married in Oxford. Now she lives in Devon with her vicar-husband and wild son, spending much of her time impersonating *Famous Five* characters and making up funny songs.

You can find her at www.TanyaMarlow.com, where she writes on the Bible, the messy edges of life and finding God in hard places. She keeps talking about making a podcast.

Follow her adventures via tinyurl.com/tanyamarlowwaits

Made in the USA
Coppell, TX
08 October 2020